THE
LITTLE
BOOK
OF
OXFORDSHIRE

PAUL SULLIVAN

The
History
Press

For Jan and Theo, sons and residents

First published 2012
This paperback edition published 2021

The History Press
97 St George's Place,
Cheltenham,
Gloucestershire,
GL50 3QB
www.thehistorypress.co.uk

British Library Cataloguing in Publication Data.
A catalogue record for this book is available from the British Library.

ISBN 978 0 7509 9732 4

Typesetting and origination by The History Press
Printed and bound by TJ Books Limited, Padstow, Cornwall

CONTENTS

	Acknowledgements	5
	Introduction	6
1.	Founders, Keepers:	9
	The People Who Shaped Oxfordshire	
2.	Town and Village	25
3.	Saints and Sinners	39
4.	The Art of Being Famous	55
5.	Crime and Punishment	76
6.	Legends, Superstition and the Supernatural	90
7.	The Working Life	109
8.	University, College and School	122
9.	Sport and Leisure	135
10.	Food and Drink	151
11.	Natural History	160
12.	Oxfordshire at War	175
	Bibliography	191

ACKNOWLEDGEMENTS

Thanks to the following: Marlene Sullivan (aka Mam) for once again giving me the time, space and three meals a day that enabled this book to be written; Terry Sullivan (aka Dad) for being part of the above, and for taking photographs; Jay Sullivan, who saw less of me as a result of all the background reading, but was the best of company when we managed to grab time together; Cate Ludlow, Jennifer Briancourt and Beth Amphlett at The History Press, who gave the go ahead and wielded the editorial shears; and Geoff Morgan and Sarah Day, who probably don't realise how encouraging they were.

INTRODUCTION

Oxfordshire is schizophrenic. Part of it likes to think of itself as the Cotswolds, another part is defined by the Chilterns, and the northern chunk calls itself Banburyshire. A large section to the south was wrested from Berkshire in 1974, and the county town's University has often dominated matters – like a sergeant-major in a room full of new recruits – leading to the 'Town and Gown' divide. But in spite of this, the county has a pleasing visual cohesion, based on low, rolling hills and swathes of agricultural land, and well-manicured structures of golden limestone and Oxfordshire bricks. It has institutions that knit it together too, from RAF bases to morris dancing, and from Civil War battlefields to Aunt Sally championships.

As an educational gateway for royalty, politicians, artists and scientists, Oxford and its satellite villages have unfair riches of celebrity residents. The history of Oxford is in many ways the history of England; but when combined with tales from the outlying towns and villages, the brew is even richer.

In the interests of space, I have had to suppress my instinct to include every theme under the sun; and if any omission seems glaring, it is simply that the stories gathered here won their place on a first-come-first-served basis. The main purpose of this book is to entertain, through insightful, funny and sometimes disturbing stories. In doing so it covers as much of the county as possible, from gleaming high streets to muddy back lanes, giving equal emphasis to each of the five Local Authority areas of Cherwell, Oxford, South Oxfordshire, Vale of White Horse and West Oxfordshire. Wherever you find yourself in the county, there is a quirky tale in this book describing something weird that can be seen or experienced, or that happened, nearby. So, to whet the appetite:

On 6 July 1696, George Fuller of Chinnor sold his wife to Thomas Heath of Thame for 2¼d per lb, like meat on a market stall. The grand total was 29s ¼d (making her just over 11 stone, or 70 kilos).

The buyer and his purchase enjoyed an illicit honeymoon at the White Hart in Benson, but were arrested after three months, fined, and forced to separate.

Grey's Court, near Rotherfield, features a donkey-powered engine. Until well into the twentieth century, the patient beasts walked around a treadmill in the Tudor-built wheel house, operating a pulley that delivered water from a well.

Despite Percy Bysshe Shelley (1792–1822) being expelled from University College for writing the pamphlet *The Necessity of Atheism*, he is now its most celebrated alumnus. The memorial statue by Edward Onslow Ford (which was given to the College when the cemetery in Rome where Shelley was buried refused to have it) depicts him nude and dead on the shore at Viareggio, where he drowned.

A flock of Chastleton geese were turned to stone by a witch, when their keeper refused to give her charity. Their remains can still be seen today in the form of an unkempt monolith and a scatter of rocks known as the Goose Stones.

Students used to feed the deer in Magdalen College Grove with a traditional snack of port-soaked sugar cubes.

The A4130, on the edge of the village of Bix, became one of England's first dual carriageways in 1937.

In 1853, a Cuddesdon resident suffering from goitre – swelling of the throat region due to a thyroid problem, usually indicative of iodine deficiency – asked for a dead man's hand to be applied to the afflicted spot. Her father's goitre had been cured by such a treatment, the swelling disappearing as the hand rotted away.

The steps and base of Leafield's Market Cross are mediaeval, but the shaft and cross were added in 1873. The new erection was an act of thanksgiving, after the village survived a smallpox epidemic – giving the monument the none-too-pretty tag of the Smallpox Cross.

Alice Liddell saw the head and feet of a dodo on a trip to the Ashmolean with Charles Dodgson. The latter, suffering a stammer, instantly became nicknamed Do-do-Dodgson, and, under his *nom de plume* Lewis Carroll, immortalised both Liddell and himself (as a dodo) in the Alice books.

An invisible phantom coach travels aimlessly but noisily up the Turnpike Road at Aston Tirrold, and a similar thing happens in the courtyard of the Crown & Thistle Hotel in Abingdon.

The stone hounds surmounting the twin pillars at the gateway of Crowsley Park House, near Henley, are effigies of the dogs kept by former owner Sir Henry Baskerville. He was High Sheriff of Oxfordshire in 1847, and his dogs are said to have been the inspiration for Arthur Conan Doyle's *The Hound of the Baskervilles*.

A man was crushed beneath his own cart wheels in 1872, when his horse reared after meeting an elephant on the road from Oxford to Eynsham.

In 1087, Saxon landowner Lady Elviva had to hand over Ambrosden to William the Conqueror's butler, Hugh d'Ivry. In the eighteenth century, it passed to the wonderfully named Page-Turner family, who I immediately invoke as patrons of this book.

Paul Sullivan
Oxford, 2012

1

FOUNDERS, KEEPERS:
The People Who Shaped Oxfordshire

LEGENDARY BEGINNINGS

Memphric

Brutus, great-grandson of Aeneus (survivor of the Siege of Troy), founded Britain around 1120 BC. Amongst his retinue were Greek philosophers, who founded a school at Greeklade (Cricklade) on the banks of the Thames. This embryonic university later shifted to Oxford (*Rydychen* in the native tongue, *Bellisitum* in Latin), a city founded by Brutus' great grandson Memphric. Memphric (aka Mempricius) was not the most inspirational of founding fathers, murdering his brother at a banquet, opting for tyranny, slaughter and sodomy, and eventually getting eaten by wolves.

The ancient and blood-stained seat of learning fell into decline after the demise of the house of Brutus in the sixth century BC. It was reduced to ashes by the Roman General Plautus in AD 50, and restored by Saxon King Alfred more than 800 years later. And, if you believe that, you'll believe anything. This was the apocrypha and wishful thinking that passed for fact in days gone by. The date of the foundation of Oxford and its University is still unknown, and although there is a strong case to be made for Alfred the Great as founder, the city only enters the written historical record in the reign of his successor.

Emperor Domitian II

Roman Emperor Domitian II cropped up on a coin unearthed in northern France in 1990. However, there was no historical record of him and the sovereign was dismissed as a fake. But, in 2003, Domitian II was resurrected after a second coin was found at Chalgrove in Oxfordshire, part of a hoard now kept by the Ashmolean Museum in Oxford.

Domitian appears to have been a third-century AD soldier elevated to emperor by his followers in Gaul and Britain, but with no official recognition elsewhere. Minting coins was a way of stamping authority, literally, on your dominions. The depiction of the minor emperor shows him with a beard and a fiery crown – representing Sol Invictus, the Invincible Sun.

King Ambrosius Aurelianus

According to local legend, Ambrosden is named after Romano-British King Ambrosius Aurelianus. He rallied the fractious Celtic tribes and succeeded in winning back the island from the invading Saxons in the first half of the fifth century AD. Treacherously poisoned, he passed the crown to his brother Uther Pendragon, who in turn handed it to his son – Ambrosius' nephew – Arthur.

Ambrosius is from a period of British history that truly counts as a Dark Age: the chronicle-free transition from Roman Britain to Anglo-Saxon England. He seems to have existed, but the links to Arthur are wishful thinking; and Ambrosden itself is probably not named after the warlord king, but from Saxon elements meaning 'Ambre's Hill'.

King Alfred and Edward the Elder

It was once believed that King Alfred died at Faringdon's Salutation Inn (presumably in the Smoke Room, given his reputation with cakes). When the historical rug was pulled from under this theory, it was claimed instead that Alfred's son Edward the Elder died there. It seems churlish to deny this one as well, but there is no evidence to back it up.

Edward the Confessor

Edward the Confessor was born in Islip around AD 1005. A thousand years later, the village celebrated this fact with various events, including a ceremonial boat-burning and a visit from Channel 4's *Time Team*. The TV archaeologists endeavoured to uncover the royal palace of Edward's father King Ethelred, plus a twelfth-century chapel dedicated to the Confessor. The latter had been knocked down in the late eighteenth century, but a detailed drawing of the building had survived, and it would surely be a relatively simple feat to uncover foundations. However, the dig turned up nothing – no palace, no chapel. Some stone walls unearthed at a promising site turned out to be a seventeenth-century cesspit, with preserved faeces intact.

MOVERS AND SHAKERS

King William and his family

After the Norman Conquest in 1066, Oxfordshire was up for grabs. Most of it went to King William's relatives: Odo of Bayeux, Robert d'Oilly and William FitzOsbern. Odo owned vast swathes in the Headington, Bampton and Wootton regions; d'Oilly received Oxford and much more besides; while FitzOsbern went on to become Earl of Hereford, Gloucester, Worcester and Oxfordshire, one of England's richest landowners and castle builders. During William's absences, FitzOsbern was effectively in charge. When he died in battle in 1070, his son Robert de Breteuil took the next obvious step and rebelled against King William. The rebellion was crushed, and he was deprived of all his lands and titles. Oxfordshire was back on the feudal merry-go-round once again.

Elyas

One of the earliest architects of Oxford was a mason called Elyas. His name appears in various city accounts, and he would have been one of the most prominent and successful non-aristocrats of his age.

First mentioned in 1187 as receiving money for work on the new royal palace of Beaumont in Oxford, by the next year Elyas was being paid daily for the upkeep of the building, in addition to his other fees. He remained keeper of Beaumont until 1200, by which time he was a rich man, working for Kings Richard I and John at locations as diverse as Porchester, Hastings, Rochester, Pevensey, Marlborough, Westminster, the New Forest, the Tower of London, and again at Oxford, where he worked on the castle. Elyas also built and managed the royal siege engines that brought victory during the Siege of Nottingham in 1194.

Alice de la Pole

Ewelme School was founded 1404–75 by Alice de la Pole, granddaughter of poet Geoffrey Chaucer. It was built with profits from the wool trade of East Anglia, where Alice raked it in as Duchess of Suffolk. It is the oldest council-run school in Britain.

Alice also built Ewelme's St Mary's Church, and almshouses which are officially called 'The Two Chaplains and Thirteen Poor Men of Ewelme in the County of Oxford'. The houses are still run as a charity by Ewelme Trust. The founder, and her father Thomas Chaucer, are buried in the church. Hers is an impressive effigy-topped tomb, with a semi-concealed 'cadaver' at its base – a life-sized statue of the departed in mid-rot, all skin and bones, all glory faded. This was a

Broughton Castle.

humble reminder to the great and good that they were, ultimately, destined for dust and decay like everyone else.

The Fiennes

The Fiennes dynasty, owners of Broughton Castle, very nearly came unstuck in the Civil War when William Fiennes supported the Parliamentarian cause, raising troops for the indecisive Battle of Edgehill in 1642. Broughton was subsequently commandeered by Charles I's men, and went into a steep decline afterwards. By the nineteenth century the castle was falling down, until Frederick Fiennes (Lord Saye and Sele) employed architect George Gilbert Scott to carry out drastic renovation.

Broughton Castle has been used as a location in many films and TV shows, including *The Madness of King George* (1994), *Shakespeare in Love* (1998) and *Jane Eyre* (2011).

Thomas Wyatt

In a bid to become royal favourite, Thomas Wyatt led an abortive rebellion in 1554 to oust Queen Mary I and install her sister Elizabeth on the throne. The latter was promptly arrested and taken to Woodstock for genteel imprisonment. Embarrassingly, Woodstock Manor was too dilapidated to accommodate her, and she was locked in the Gatehouse instead.

Francis Knollys

Francis Knollys (d. 1596) was a leading political figure under Tudor monarchs Henry VIII, Edward VI and Elizabeth I, having evaded Catholic Mary I by going into exile. He lived at Grey's Court near Rotherfield Greys, whose church has an eye-popping monument depicting Francis, his wife (who was a cousin of Henry VIII's second wife Anne Boleyn), and fourteen of his children. His eldest son, another Francis, was MP for Oxford in the late sixteenth century, and gained much of his wealth through State-sanctioned piracy, like his good friend Sir Francis Drake. Knolly's heraldic symbol, a black elephant, decorates the Oxford coat of arms in the company of a green beaver, a lion, and the eponymous ox. MP for Reading until his death at the age of ninety in 1648, he was described by the Governor of Reading, Sir Arthur Aston, as 'the ancientest Parliament man in England'.

John Radcliffe

John Radcliffe never saw the Radcliffe Camera. The Oxford landmark was funded with money bequeathed by him in 1714 to house a medical library (Radcliffe being the physician who opened the city's first infirmary, and after whom the modern John Radcliffe Hospital is named). The Camera was built by James Gibbs between 1737 and 1749, after he triumphed against Nicholas Hawksmoor for the honour. It is the most iconic – and photographed – structure in the city, at the heart of the cobbled Radcliffe Square, with Colleges and University cathedral glowing all around in Cotswold stone.

The Radcliffe Camera and Library.

Radcliffe Square.

HIGH SHERIFF OF OXFORDSHIRE

Edwin

Sheriffs – shire-reeves – originated as the King's direct representatives in the shires, and were responsible for squeezing every last penny of taxation from the overburdened populace, and for upholding law and order. The first named High Sheriff of Oxfordshire was the Saxon Edwin, who steered the county from the 1066 conquest through to Domesday in 1086. Normans held the title from then on.

Falkes de Breauté

Notable High Sheriffs include the splendidly named Manasser Arsick (1160–2), and Falkes de Breauté (1215–23). Falkes was a loyal defender of Kings John and Henry III, and his heraldic symbol was a griffin. His London residence was called Falke's Hall, which became Fawkes Hall, then Foxhall, Fauxhall and, finally, Vauxhall. Vauxhall cars began production at Vauxhall Ironworks, London, in 1903, and in a time-defying piece of symbolism, the company still uses Falkes de Breauté's griffin as its heraldic badge.

Thomas Chaucer

Between 1248 and 1566, the High Sheriff of Oxfordshire title was held jointly with that of High Sheriff of Berkshire. Amongst its notable holders was Thomas Chaucer (in office 1400–3), son of famed poet Geoffrey. He owned the manors of Ewelme and Woodstock, and carried impressive additional titles such as Speaker of the House of Commons; Chief Butler for England; Constable of Wallingford Castle; Steward of the Honours of Wallingford, St Valery and the Chiltern Hundreds; and MP for Oxfordshire (1400–31). He was active at the Battle of Agincourt in 1415, served as a royal householder to Henry V, and was a member of the royal council under Henry VI. He died fabulously wealthy at Ewelme on 18 November 1434, aged sixty-seven. But in spite of all this, he was still accosted in the street with: 'Hey, didn't your dad write *The Canterbury Tales?*'

Richard Taverner

Richard Taverner, who produced an English translation of the Bible, was High Sheriff in 1569. As a young man, he had read Tyndale's outlawed English Bible in Oxford, and was arrested for doing so; but the religious seeds were sown. Prior to being Sheriff he was a lay preacher, renowned for his flowery speeches. He once told a congregation at St Mary's in Oxford: 'I have brought you some fine biscuits baked in the oven of charity, carefully conserved for the chickens of the church, the sparrows of the spirit, and the sweet swallows of salvation.'

Sir Anthony Cope

Sir Anthony Cope was Sheriff three times between 1581 and 1603. A Protestant zealot, he was imprisoned in the Tower of London for a month in 1587 when, as MP for Banbury, he presented the Speaker of the Commons with a Puritan version of the Book of Common Prayer and a Bill attacking Church law. This served him well when the ecclesiastical tide turned: he was knighted by Elizabeth I in 1590 and became a baronet under James I in 1611. (Baronets were invented by James I to raise money: title holders had to fork out for the

Hanwell Castle.

honour.) Cope died magnificently wealthy in 1614, aged sixty-six, and was buried on his estate at Hanwell.

Female High Sheriffs
The first female High Sheriff of Oxfordshire was Isabella Juliet Hutchinson in 1984, and women have been elected regularly ever since, including Marie-Jane Barnett in 2010 and Penelope Glen in 2011.

BLENHEIM PALACE AND ITS RESIDENTS

Dukes and Duchesses of Marlborough
Blenheim Palace in the parish of Bladon was begun by John Churchill, 1st Duke of Marlborough, in 1705 and completed in 1724 – a gift 'from the nation' for his pre-eminent role in securing victory in Bavaria at the Battle of Blenheim in 1704. The battle was a turning point in the Spanish War of Succession – even though it had another ten years to run – in which England was defending Habsburg Emperor Leopold's HQ at Vienna against the forces of Louis XIV of France. Thirty thousand French troops died at Blenheim, and the seemingly inexorable advance of a Roman Empire-style French Europe was effectively halted on that day. Marlborough went on to enjoy other famous victories at Ramillies in 1706, Oudenarde in 1708 and Malplaquet in 1709, by which time he was national hero bar none.

Queen Anne was a close friend to Sarah, the Duchess of Marlborough – but the 'gift from the nation' became increasingly grudging when the two women fell out. Their last clash occurred in 1711, after which Anne cancelled the Blenheim funds.

Things had never run smoothly on the enormous building site (where the ruins of Woodstock Palace had been swept away on the whim of the Duchess). The Duke had ignored the credentials of Christopher Wren, the obvious man for the job of building the palace, and opted for the playwright John Vanbrugh, an untrained architect who had recently worked with Nicholas Hawksmoor on Harewood House in Yorkshire. Going solo, Vanbrugh's designs were criticised from the outset, and used as a lever in Parliament to stem the flow of cash. The Duchess had disapproved of the architect from the start; but now she hated him.

With the money dried up, the royals disowning them and the whole project turning into a white elephant, the Churchills were forced into exile in 1714, owing the builders a huge sum. It was the year

Royal palace of Woodstock.

the Spanish War of Succession finished, ironically, and Marlborough's star should have been at its zenith.

Once Queen Anne was underground and George I was installed, the Marlboroughs were back in favour. Vanbrugh was sacked and Hawksmoor finished Blenheim, whose construction was now financed entirely by the Duke. In 1725, Vanbrugh visited the recently completed palace as a member of the public, but was turned away at the gate.

Blenheim – one of largest houses in the country – is the only non-royal or Church-related house to bear the title 'Palace'. Since 1987 it has been a UNESCO World Heritage Site, and its vast interiors and idiosyncratic gardens, follies, maze and other tourist-pleasers, make it the county's main hotspot outside Oxford itself.

Lord Robert Spencer
As reported in *Jackson's Oxford Journal*, on 3 April 1762:

> ... Lord Robert Spencer, youngest brother to his Grace the Duke of Marlborough, most providentially escaped being suffocated, and burnt in his Bed, at Blenheim House in this County. His Lordship waking suddenly, almost Two o'clock in the Morning, found the Curtains of his Bed, the Hangings of the Room, a Chest of Drawers, and other Pieces of Furniture in Flames, and the room filled with Smoak ... The Fire was happily extinguished, without spreading

any further. ... A Powder Flask had taken Fire, the explosion of which most probably first disturbed his Lordship. This Accident cannot be accounted for, unless a Spark might have fallen from the Candle among the Linen, while the Servant was putting it up in the Drawers, the Evening before.

Winston Churchill

Blenheim's most famous son is Sir Winston Leonard Spencer-Churchill, who shares a grave with his wife Clementine in St Martin's churchyard, Bladon. Amongst his many claims to fame, he is the only prime minister to have received the Nobel Prize for Literature ('History will be kind to me, for I intend to write it'), and to have been made an honorary citizen of the USA. Legend says that he was born in a toilet at Blenheim: the Duchess had gone into labour early during an evening dance, having suffered a fall during the afternoon shooting party. Winston's words on the subject were: 'Although present on the occasion, I have no clear recollection of the event.'

Amongst Churchill's less successful projects were the ill-fated Gallipoli Campaign in the First World War (while he was First Lord of the Admiralty), and his opposition to the abdication of national liability Edward VIII in 1936. More successfully, he was a war correspondent, reporting from the heart of conflict in such diverse 1890s' arenas as Cuba (in which he acquired his lifelong taste for Havana cigars), the Indian Siege of Malakand, the Boer War in South Africa and the re-conquest of Sudan. While in South Africa he was imprisoned as a POW, and escaped via a 480km trek to Portuguese-held Delagoa Bay. Undeterred, he later returned to the fray and was instrumental in key victories at Pretoria. He wrote various books and articles detailing his heroic experiences. And all this before entering Parliament for the first time in 1900!

Always larger than life and supremely self-confident, Churchill naturally ran up against a few detractors:

> Lady Nancy Astor: If I were your wife I would put poison in your coffee.
> Churchill: Nancy, if I were your husband, I would drink it.

But on the whole, the admirers outnumbered them:

> Female fan admiring new sculpture of Winston: Mr Churchill, I want you to know that I got up at dawn and drove a hundred miles for the unveiling of your bust.

Churchill: Madam, I want you to know that I would happily reciprocate the honour.

Churchill's death on 30 January 1965 was greeted by national mourning ('I am ready to meet my maker. Whether my maker is prepared for the ordeal of meeting me is another matter'). His body was taken to Hanborough railway station by a locomotive called, appropriately enough, *Winston Churchill*, and the funeral procession continued by road to Bladon.

Alva Vanderbilt

The county's most spectacular arranged marriage occurred in 1896. Fabulously rich American heiress, Alva Vanderbilt, noted the down-at-heel aspect of Blenheim Palace and contacted the current owner, Charles, 9th Duke of Marlborough.

Alva had just the thing to reverse Marlborough's failing fortunes: her daughter Consuelo. The Duke agreed, negotiating a £2.5 million dowry; but Consuelo had set her heart on another man. Alva, threatening to murder her daughter's lover, locked Consuelo in her room before the wedding, fearing an elopement.

The marriage took place in New York, and afterwards the Duke declared that he hated all things non-British, would never return to America, and loved another woman. Blenheim was bailed out, but the relationship was a non-starter; and, after their divorce in 1921, the Duke married another American woman, a friend of Consuelo's. The former Duchess, having shocked society in 1906 by walking out on her husband, lived to see her son John become 10th Duke of Marlborough. She died in 1964.

KINGS AND QUEENS

The sixth and seventh-century Kings of Mercia had a court at Benson – Oxfordshire being on their war-torn border with Wessex.

King Cynegils was baptised at Dorchester-on-Thames, and his son Cwichelm had a similar encounter with holy water in AD 636, dying in the same year.

Edwold, brother of East Anglian King Edmund, turned down the offer of the crown when Edmund was murdered in AD 869, retiring instead to the embryonic monastic community at Dorchester.

The Market Cross, Woodstock.

Ethelred I had a royal court at Woodstock, 865–71.

Ethelred's son, **Alfred the Great** (reigned 871–99), may have founded Oxford University. He was born at Wantage, and is said to have convened one of the first English parliaments at Shifford.

Alfred's son, **Edward the Elder** (reigned 899–924), is the first king with verifiable links to Oxford. His brother and his son, Kings Ethelward and Athelstan, lived and studied here too.

Ethelred II 'the Unready' (968–1013) held councils at Oxford, Woodstock and Eynsham, and had further palaces at Islip and Headington.

Danish **King Sweyn** burned down Oxford during the single year of his reign in England in 1013 (a feat which the Danes repeated in 1032).

Edmund II (Ironside) was murdered at Oxford in 1016 after a seven-month reign.

Canute, son of King Sweyn, resided in Oxford and held many councils there during his reign, 1016–35.

Harold I (Harefoot) was crowned in Oxford in 1035.

Edward the Confessor (reigned 1042–66) was born at Islip in 1004.

William the Conqueror stormed Oxford in 1067.

Henry I (d. 1135), the Conqueror's son, earned the nickname Beauclerc through his patronage of Oxford. He founded Beaumont Palace here and rebuilt the palace at Woodstock, installing a walled park and menagerie. These two sites were the seats of many monarchs to come.

King Stephen (d. 1154) and his niece **Matilda** (d. 1141) planned and staged much of their civil warring in Oxford in the twelfth century.

Both **King Richard I** and **King John** were born at Beaumont in the mid-twelfth century.

Sometime residents of Beaumont and/or Woodstock include **Henry II** (d. 1189), **Henry III** (d. 1272) and **Edward I** (d. 1307). The latter's son **Edmund** was born at Woodstock in 1301, as was **Edward the Black Prince**, son of **Edward III**, in 1330, and his brother **Thomas 'of Woodstock'** in 1355.

Henry III spent Christmas at Osney Abbey in 1222 'with great revelling mirth'.

Most monarchs from **Henry II** onwards were benefactors of the University. **Edward III** (reigned 1327–77) was a great patron, setting the trend.

Richard II (reigned 1377–99) held Christmas and other festivities at Woodstock, and **Henry IV** (d. 1413) was based here, and at Beaumont, too. His son **Henry V** (d. 1422) was a student at Queen's College.

Edward IV (1442–70) lived in the palace at Langley, with its access to the royal hunting grounds of Wychwood Forest. He assumed the title Protector of the University of Oxford.

Richard III (reigned 1483–5) held courts at Magdalen College prior to the winter of his discontent.

Henry VII (d. 1509) favoured Woodstock Palace and its hunting grounds, and his son Arthur was born here. His successor, **Henry VIII** (reigned 1509–47), favoured London, but was forced to live at

Abingdon in 1518 to avoid the 'sweating sickness'. Henry also used the palace at Woodstock, founded Christ Church College, and made Oxford the centre of one of six new Bishoprics.

Mary I's association with Oxford is chiefly through the martyrdom of unrepentantly non-Catholic Bishops Ridley and Cranmer, 1555/6.

Elizabeth I was kept under house arrest at Woodstock while her sister Mary reigned, and, as queen (1558–1603), she lived briefly at Rycote. She was very fond of Oxford and its University.

James I moved to Oxford to avoid the London plague in 1603, and his son, **Charles I**, famously chose Oxford as his base during the ill-starred wars that ended with his beheading in 1649. He also resided at Woodstock and Rycote.

Charles II avoided the London plague at Oxford 1665–6.

James II (deposed 1688) used Oxford as the base for his resurgent Catholicism, University College being used for Roman Catholic Mass.

William III held court at Henley-on-Thames prior to taking up the throne in 1689. He enjoyed support in the county, notably during his stay at Burford.

Queen Anne was a frequent visitor to Oxford, and it was she who gave the ancient royal estate at Woodstock to the Dukes of Marlborough in 1704.

The Georgian era had a rocky start in Oxfordshire, much of the county supporting the Stuart claim to the throne. The Hanoverians' main mark on the county is the statue of **Queen Caroline** at Queen's College. She was the wife of **George II** (reigned 1727–60) and benefactress of the College.

George III's father, **Frederick, Prince of Wales**, visited Wroxton Abbey in 1739; an obelisk in its park commemorates the fact. It also notes visits from **George IV** in the early nineteenth century.

George III (reigned 1760–1820) was a regular visitor to Nuneham Park, and rekindled the royal connection with Oxford.

Queen Victoria (reigned 1837–1901) was frequently wined and dined in the county.

WHO'S IN CHARGE NOW?

When taxation finally made it to the upper echelons of society, county councils and the likes of the National Trust purchased many large estates and houses from their cash-strapped owners. Various rich celebrities have moved in too. The Colleges of Oxford University still own much of the city and county, though, and a few other rich landlords battle on. The Dukes of Marlborough still own Blenheim, and Lord and Lady Saye and Sele rule the roost at Broughton Castle.

But the strangest roost is at Faringdon House, where the pigeons are dyed bright colours. 'Mistrust a man who never has an occasional flash of silliness,' said the Right Honourable Sir Gerald Hugh Tyrwhitt-Wilson, aka the 14th Lord Berners (1883–1950), minor composer, novelist and painter, and owner of Faringdon House. He is responsible for the extant tradition of pigeon-dyeing. He was also fond of erecting signs along the lines of: 'Do not throw stones at this notice' and 'Mangling done here' – the latter inscribed on a plaque on the door of Faringdon House.

Berners' output includes the immortal verse:

Red Roses blow but thrice a year,
In June, July or May:
But owners of Red Noses
Can blow them every day.

The county's most infamous rich resident was Robert Maxwell, the newspaper magnate found guilty of stealing money from pension fund schemes. Maxwell died in 1991 in suspicious circumstances, whilst yachting off the Canary Islands. The official verdict of accidental death has been countered by theories of murder and suicide. He lived at Headington Hill Hall, although he never actually owned it. It was leased from Oxford City Council, and dubbed the most expensive council house in the world. The site is now occupied by Oxford Brookes University. Maxwell is buried on the Mount of Olives in Jerusalem.

Kiddington Hall, built in 1673, had its first makeover when Lancelot 'Capability' Brown laid out new gardens in the mid-eighteenth century. A hundred years later, the architect Charles Barry controversially remodelled the entire hall, leaving no trace of the original exterior. In the 1950s, the hall was bought by the Robson family, founders of chartered accountancy firm Robson Rhodes. But in 2009 the owner put it, and the larger Kiddington estate (more than 1,600 acres, largely the village of Nether Kiddington, including its eighteen houses and kindergarten, and another twenty-odd buildings), on the market for £42 million. After much media speculation, the hall section of the portfolio was bought in 2010 by heiress Jemima Goldsmith.

Glympton House was bought by King Abdullah of Saudi Arabia's nephew Prince Bandar, Saudi Ambassador to the US, in 1992. The £8 million sale price was inflated by the £40 million that needed spending on renovation and security (such as bullet-proof glass). Prince Bandar has since bought another 500 acres of surrounding land.

But it's not all about money and ownership. Shute Barrington, Bishop of Durham, founded the country's first co-operative shop. He was born in Shrivenham and educated at Merton College. The ground-breaking shop opened in 1794 at Mongewell, selling locally produced bacon, cheese and other basics at rock-bottom, no-middle-man prices. Shoppers were able to save an estimated 21 per cent.

Barrington went on to publish utopian plans for co-operative and social life, 'far exceeding in variety and thoroughness any in the minds of persons now living', as social commentator George Jacob wrote, sixty years after the co-op king's death. He added:

> Co-operation was born of the feeling that unmitigated competition is at best but social war; and though war has its great conquests, its pomps, its bards, its proud associations and heroic memories, there is murder in its march; and humanity and genius were things to blush for, if progress cannot be accomplished by some nobler means. What an enduring truce is to war, co-operation is to the never-ceasing conflict between capital and labour. It is the peace of industry.

And it all started in Mongewell, better known today for being one of the many scenic locations traversed by the Ridgeway long-distance footpath.

2

TOWN AND VILLAGE

ANCIENT AND RUINED

Bones

Local legend says that, during a storm, a man rode his horse across Blewburton Hill between Aston Upthorpe and Blewbury. There was an enormous clap of thunder, and rider and horse simply disappeared, hammered into the ground by the thunderbolt. The tale may be linked to the remains of ten 3,000-year-old horses discovered during archaeological excavations at the Iron Age site in the 1940s. They were probably bludgeoned and buried here to appease the gods, and to defend the walls in the form of vengeful spirits.

This notion of an undead defence force was widespread. The remains of a dog and a man, discovered in the foundations of a Romano-British wall at the Churchill kilns near Headington in Oxford, are a case in point. The dog was supposed to take ghostly bites at the legs of would-be intruders, while the wraith of the man threw a few sticks during history's quieter periods.

Roman villa

In 1812, the remains of a Roman villa were discovered at North Leigh near Witney. At the time of its occupation, the fourth-century villa had four bath suites, sixteen mosaic floors and eleven rooms with under-floor heating, all of which were abandoned when the Romans withdrew from Britain 100 years later.

News of the archaeological sensation spread quickly, and souvenir hunters were ruthless. A few years after its discovery, two of the three surviving mosaic floors had been stolen tile by tile. Site owner, the Duke of Marlborough, erected a damage-limitation shed over the surviving one, and it can still be seen in its fragmentary glory, under the custodianship of English Heritage. In its heyday, it would have been one of the largest Roman villas on the island.

Hampton Gay Manor

There were no Portakabins in the eighteenth century when John Vanburgh was building Blenheim Palace. The place where he took his lunch break was the Elizabethan Hampton Gay Manor in Kidlington. His contribution to that lowlier but still impressive edifice was the towered outside loo in the front garden, which still stands.

Hampton Gay Manor has been through various private hands, but fell into disrepair after a devastating fire in 1887. This was said to be the result of a curse laid on the house when its occupants refused to shelter victims of the Paddington-to-Birkenhead Express, which derailed nearby in 1874. Since then, the manor has looked like a film set for a Gothic horror; but plans are finally afoot to help the ruin rise from the ashes.

The environs of Hampton Gay Manor have seen many famous residents, including Civil War era Royalist and Judge Sir William Morton, and nineteenth-century social reform advocate John Pudsey Welchman Sydenham, who came to national attention during the period of local unrest known as the Otmoor Riots. Medicine man Thomas Beecham lived in a cottage nearby when he formulated the powders and pills that would make him famous. He was working as gardener to the manor at the time.

Brightwell Park House

Brightwell Park House, built in 1790 – its famed ballroom stretching the full length of the vast upper floor – fell down in the early twentieth century. The previous manor house here at Brightwell Baldwin had burnt down; its successor had chosen an alternative element to foment its destruction: damp rot. A Grade II listed seventeenth-century dovecote, shaped like a Greek cross, survived the ruin.

ALL CHANGE

In 1974, Oxfordshire devoured a huge chunk of Berkshire, gaining well over 100 settlements. These Johnny-come-latelys include Abingdon, Didcot, Faringdon, Wallingford, Wantage, Wytham, and Oxford suburbs Botley, South Hinksey and Harcourt Hill.

Counties (Detached Parts) Act

These were not the first to be subsumed or spat out by the fickle county. Village transmigration occurred in 1844 with the Counties (Detached Parts) Act shuffling settlements between Oxfordshire and its neighbours Berkshire, Buckinghamshire, Gloucestershire and Warwickshire. One Oxfordshire gain was Widford, which had been an isolated chunk of Gloucestershire surrounded on all sides by its new home county. Subsequent nineteenth-century Local Government Acts continued the shuffling, and the last shifts were in 1991, when unpopulated bits on the Bucks/Berks/Oxon borders quietly swapped sides.

Mollington

Mollington has managed to be in three counties. It was originally part of Oxfordshire, Northamptonshire and Warwickshire. A few hundred years ago it lost the Northants bit, and in 1895 the remaining Warwicks part got swallowed by Oxfordshire.

Abingdon

The County Hall building in Abingdon (currently a museum), perched on pillars and arches, was designed by seventeenth-century Burford-born stonemason Christopher Kempster, who had chiselled his way to expertise with Christopher Wren on the building of St Paul's Cathedral in London. He later produced one of Oxford's jewels – Tom Tower at Christ Church College.

Christ Church Tom Tower.

Kempster's County Hall was built when Abingdon was the county town of Berkshire – a position it held until 1867, when Reading usurped it. Now in Oxfordshire, it is unique in being a former county town that has since shifted to another county.

Town Hall in Faringdon
The old Town Hall in Faringdon has the rare distinction of never having been a town hall at all. At various times it has been a market office, a gaol, a police station, a library, a fire station, a charity shop and a meeting room.

East Hagbourne
East Hagbourne suffered catastrophe in 1659 when most of its houses were lost in a fire, their thatched roofs the perfect fuel. Charles II was petitioned for aid, and in 1661 money was raised from Londoners and sent to the village to assist the rebuilding. The surviving timber-framed beauties from this era are testimony to money well spent.

But the story did not end there. In 1666, when London suffered an even more drastic version of the Great Fire of East Hagbourne, the villagers reciprocated by sending money to help the city rebuild itself.

Another demolition may be on its way, though. A pending proposal to build a south Didcot bypass could mean losing a chunk of East Hagbourne, including most of its New Road area. Perhaps another petition to London is in order.

Chastleton House
After years of decay, the Jacobean house at Chastleton is now a treasured time capsule: National Trust publicity lures you in by boasting of 'a kitchen ceiling last cleaned in 1612'. The rules of croquet were first codified at Chastleton House in 1865.

Cogges Manor
In the early 1970s, thirteenth-century Cogges Manor in the village of Cogges near Witney was a true throwback – a self-supporting manor providing work, food and shelter for residents, staff and labourers. Oxfordshire County Council bought the site in 1974, and from then until 2009 Cogges Manor Farm was a working museum, on the same lines as before but this time as a tourist attraction.

Chastleton dovecote.

The site is now run by the Cogges Agricultural Heritage Museum Trust, and, in the summer of 2011, with an army of volunteers and a huge wave of goodwill, the farm reopened.

Kingston Bagpuize

Kingston Bagpuize is named after Ralph de Bagpuis, who came a-looting with William the Conqueror in 1066. It is pronounced 'bag-pews' rather than the very tempting 'bagpuss', and was renamed Bagpipes in the Second World War by USAF airmen stationed here. The parish's full title is Kingston Bagpuize with Southmoor, the two villages being one. Southmoor has the dubious honour of having been owned by absentee landlords for more than 1,000 years – Abingdon Abbey originally, and currently St John's College, Oxford.

Mixbury

Estate owners have been able to do whatever they please throughout history. For example, Mixbury, on the Northamptonshire border, was completely demolished by decree of the Court of Chancery in 1874, at the request of the local squire. Its dilapidated rubble-stone thatched cottages were replaced with the brick-fronted 'model village' estate cottages that survive today.

Middleton Stoney and Middleton Park

Middleton Stoney near Bicester used to be in what is now Middleton Park. In 1824, landowner George Child Villiers, 5th Earl of Jersey, demolished the entire village (apart from the church and castle mound) in order to extend his garden. His wife Sarah, Countess of Jersey, ordered the building of new cottages at the edge of the new park, giving each one a porch and flower garden as compensation for the disruption.

The current Middleton Park House was rebuilt in 1938 by Edward Lutyens, commissioned by the 9th Earl of Jersey. The Earl then decided to give the house to the National Trust, but they turned it down (an illustration of how Lutyens' work, architectural gold dust these days, has since been reassessed). The property was requisitioned by the army in the Second World War and used by Polish airmen. It was converted to flats after the Jerseys sold up after the war, but is still intact – the last house of the old 'stately home' school to be built in England.

Great Tew Park

Since the 1960s, Great Tew Park has been transformed from a near-derelict estate to an award-winning farm and community. Much of the work occurred in the 1980s, when even the old ironstone quarry reopened for business. As a private estate with farmers, cottagers and church, it is an anachronism; and yet Great Tew also manages to embody the spirit of the twenty-first century with its diversity and enterprise, hosting events such as horse trials, shooting and car rallies.

Buckland

Buckland is an estate village, created to house the staff who worked at Buckland House. The current house was built in the 1750s, and has seen much redevelopment and changes of use. It was owned by Oxford University in 1963, and was bought by Formula 1 star Patrick McNally in 2004, whose plans for its future include making it a nursing home.

Carterton

William Carter bought land from the Duke of Marlborough in 1900, selling parcels of it to people who wanted to build houses for themselves. This was the origin of Carterton, Oxfordshire's 'New Town'. It got off to a poor start, with neighbouring Black Bourton perversely hindering attempts to have running water and electricity supplied to the new settlement. Prior to the Second World War, its main contribution to the economy was locally grown tomatoes. Some of these Carterton fruits sank in the kitchens of the *Titanic* in 1912.

Faringdon

During the Second World War, the 43m-high tower on Faringdon (or Folly) Hill was used by the Home Guard as a lookout post, affording views across the surrounding Vale of the White Horse. It was built as a folly in 1935 by landowner Lord Berners, who little suspected the practical use it would be put to a few years later. In 1982, Robert Heber-Percy restored the tower and donated it to the town of Faringdon. The hill upon which it stands was already a local landmark: its still-thriving Scots pines were planted by the owners of Faringdon House in the eighteenth century; Cromwell fortified it in the seventeenth; Empress Matilda did something similar 500 years earlier; and it was originally an Iron Age fort (like nearby Badbury Hill) on a prominent Greensand outcrop.

Welsh links – Oxford and Cornwell

Oxfordshire's most famous connection with Wales is in Oxford: Jesus College has long had associations with Welsh scholars, and the Morris car factory employed countless Welshmen, many of them living in the purpose-built Florence Park estate. But there is a more obscure Welsh link in Cornwell. In 1939, architect Sir Bertram Clough Williams-Ellis restored the village's seventeenth-century manor house, remodelled the village's cottages and transformed the old school into a village hall. Williams-Ellis' most celebrated work had been carried out in the 1920s on the Welsh coast, where he designed the entire village of Portmeirion, an eccentric mixture of Italianate houses and follies, famously used as the location for the 1960s' TV series *The Prisoner*.

Botley

Botley has Oxford's most westerly 'dreaming spire', Seacourt Tower. The metal structure on the former car showroom, built 1965–6, gives the building the semi-affectionate local name 'Botley Cathedral'. It is not the city's newest spire, though: that accolade goes to the blunt green structure on the tower of Saïd Business School. Opened in 1996, the school features a rooftop amphitheatre, the scene of theatrical productions in the summer.

Headington

A 7m fibreglass great white shark called 'Untitled 1986' juts from the roof of a Victorian house in New High Street, Headington. It was installed by Radio Oxford DJ and former Balliol law student Bill Heine in 1986, unveiled on the forty-first anniversary of the dropping of the atomic bomb on Nagasaki. It was created by sculptor John Buckley, and has survived city council attempts to get it condemned. The shark has become the unofficial emblem of Headington.

Bill Heine's other contribution to the skyline was a set of giant hands and cancan legs installed on the roof of Headington's 'Not the Moulin Rouge' cinema in 1980. The cinema closed in 1991, and the legs were marched off to another cinema owned by Heine in Brighton. Ironically, a planning officer who had opposed the legs when they first kicked off in Headington was now a planning officer in Brighton, out on a limb once again.

M40

In a trend begun by the prehistoric Ridgeway and Icknield Way, the M40 is the latest means of making speedy progress in the county, linking Oxford with London. The southern section was constructed between 1967 and 1974, with the section between Oxford and Birmingham completed in 1990.

Its birth had not been easy. Protesters mauled the original plans, which involved the wholesale destruction of one of Oxfordshire's jewels of recreated wilderness, Otmoor. Part of the ultimately successful campaign against the original route involved selling more than 3,000 small sections of a field to worldwide buyers to raise funds. The piecemeal field had been evocatively named Alice's Field, in reference to local author Lewis Carroll and his famous literary creation.

The construction of the M40 brought consolation in the form of archaeological investigations. The Roman road Akeman Street, just west of Chesterton, was unearthed, as were Saxon graves at Postcombe, and a Romano-British settlement and cemetery at Lewknor, which also yielded a mediaeval farmhouse.

RUN OF THE MILL

Chinnor Mill has avoided the usual fate of disused windmills – i.e. demolition or conversion – in a unique manner. Built around 1750, the post mill was saved from ruin in 1966, when mill preservationists dismantled it and sent it to Norfolk. In the 2000s it was brought back, and re-erected by the Chinnor Windmill Restoration Society. It can be seen in a playing field alongside Mill Lane, on the north-west edge of the village.

A handful of other remnants are still flying the flag of Windy Miller:

Bloxham Grove Mill, a small post mill dating from 1865, stands alone in a field south of Bloxham Grove Road.

Great Haseley's tawny tower mill dates from around 1760. It is currently being renovated and can be seen south of the A329 between Great Haseley and Great Milton.

Faring less well is **North Leigh Mill**, built in 1833 by enterprising miller-cum-baker Joseph Shepherd. It was restored in 1881 and 1933, but was losing its cap in 1940 when the structure was used as an observation post during the Second World War. It awaits the saviours of restoration.

Wardington's post mill (no sails, privately owned) was built on top of a watermill in 1715.

Littleworth Mill at Wheatley is open to the public – but not very often (currently eight or so times a year). It is lovingly cared for by Wheatley Windmill Restoration Society; its octagonal tower and four gleaming new sails look magnificent.

Dozens of others have not been so lucky. **Arncott Mill** collapsed in 1950; **Chinnor**'s other mill was dismantled in advanced decay in 1965; **Bicester**'s was blown down in a gale in 1881; and **Nettlebed**'s – relocated here from its original site in Watlington in 1825 – burnt down in 1912.

On a similar translocation theme, the 1719 mill at **Cropredy** was mysteriously relocated to Avon Dassett in Warwickshire in 1725.

Sydenham's followed suit in 1801, moving to Stone in Buckinghamshire just seven years after being restored.

Wessex Mill in Wantage is still milling flour, using 1930s' machinery in a 1980s' building. It is run by a family who first put their noses to the grindstone at Oxford's **Osney Mill** (recently redeveloped as flats).

WATERWORKS

The Maharajah's Well
One good turn deserves another, according to the mid-nineteenth-century Maharajah of Benares (modern Varanasi) in India. Edward Anderson Reade, owner of Ipsden House near Henley and Governor of India's North-West Provinces, had assisted the Maharajah in 1831, using his engineering and surveying skills to bring water to the drought-plagued community of Azamgarh. The wealthy Indian leader showed his appreciation by commissioning Reade and the Wallingford firm of R.J. & H. Wilder to sink a well near Reade's home in the village of Stoke Row, which had problems with water supply. The Maharajah's Well is still the pride of the village, with its golden dome, decorative golden elephant, and shaft of 111m – a depth more than twice the length of the tallest building in Oxford (which is Magdalen College's tower, at a mere 44m).

Earl Harcourt
The Harcourts of Stanton Harcourt took over the Nuneham Courtney estate in 1710, and in the 1750s they demolished the entire village and rebuilt it a mile away, to stop it spoiling the views across the newly planned house and park.

The park was redesigned by 'Capability' Brown in the 1790s, and was going to include a neo-Gothic tower overlooking the Thames. But when Oxford University removed the ornate 1612 Carfax Conduit drinking fountain from the central crossroads of Oxford, the Harcourts used that as their tower instead. It can still be seen in the grounds.

In September 1777, a newspaper reported that Earl Harcourt had been found dead in a well in the park. 'It is imagined this melancholy accident was occasioned by his overreaching himself, in endeavouring to save the life of a favourite dog, which was found in the well with him, standing on his lordship's feet.'

William Edward Harcourt sold Nuneham Courtney to Oxford University in 1948, which used part of it as a rural annex to its Botanical Gardens. This oasis of trees, flower meadows and sandwich-snaffling peacocks, Harcourt Arboretum, is based on a pinetum (a plantation of pine trees) established in the 1830s.

Trow Pool

The 1909 water tower at Trow Pool near Bucknell, best viewed as you whizz down the M40, is now a Grade II listed building. Towers such as this are storage containers for drinking water, kept at a height to enable natural hydrostatic pressure to sloosh the water through pipes and taps, and with sufficient volume to cope with peak water usage times. Electric pumps refill water towers these days; but, even in times of power cuts, they can continue to deliver pressurised water – as long as the tower doesn't empty before the power comes back on. The constant draining and refilling also prevents the water from freezing in cold weather.

Watermills

There are some fine working watermills to be seen in the county:

Mapledurham's is the most impressive – a largely seventeenth-century structure in the grounds of Mapledurham House, and the last operational watermill on the River Thames. It has had a few brushes with fame, including a key role in the film *The Eagle Has Landed* (1976), and pride of place on Black Sabbath's debut album in 1970.

The mill at **Sonning Eye** has been converted to a theatre-cum-restaurant, and maintains its links with the past by using a small hydroelectric (water-powered) generator. It ceased milling in 1969, up to which time it had produced flour for Huntley & Palmers biscuits.

Combe Mill is an old sawmill in good working order, with a beam engine complementing the original water wheel. It is between Combe and Long Hanborough on the Evenlode, and is open as a museum.

The old watermill at **Goring-on-Thames** is still very picturesque, although it no longer churns the waters. It has been converted into an art gallery.

The one at Garford – **Venn Mill** on Childrey Brook, situated at a Roman road crossing – dates from 1800, but is only open occasionally due to that intimidating ogre of modern pastimes and sightseeing: Health and Safety.

Charney Bassett Water Mill dates back to the thirteenth century. It has not turned since the 1900s, and has been the subject of ongoing restoration since the mid-'70s. It hopes to open soon as a tourist attraction.

Dandridge's Mill in East Hanney is a former Georgian silk mill, Grade II listed, and converted to private flats in 2007. It maintains its link with the millstream, however, powering the properties' electricity generator via an Archimedean screw system.

TREASURES

The Alfred Jewel

'*Alfred mec heht gewyrcan*' (Alfred had me made) is inscribed on the dragon-headed relic known as the Alfred Jewel. It was discovered in Somerset in 1693, and bequeathed to Oxford University by its first owner, Colonel Nathaniel Palmer (1661–1718). The Jewel is thought to have been created at the command of ninth-century King Alfred the Great, perhaps as the handle of a rod, or as a small staff used for pointing to words in a book whilst reading. It can be marvelled at in the Ashmolean Museum.

Moulsford Torc

A spot of routine rotavating at Moulsford in 1960 unearthed the 3,200-year-old Moulsford Torc – a neck-ring, or torque, made of interwoven strips of gold. It was not declared Treasure Trove (and therefore did not automatically belong to the reigning monarch) due to the fact that it was a 'casual loss' rather than a deliberate treasure burial. It was sold to Reading Museum.

Lovernianus' Roman treasure

In 1968, a piece of Roman pewter was taken to the Ashmolean Museum in Oxford. It had come from a gravel pit at Appleford-on-Thames, where workmen had dredged up what looked like a pile of blackened, bent hubcaps and dustbin lids. Museum staff intervened in time to salvage eighteen pewter plates, bowls and a flagon – a total later added to by pieces that had been ghosted away by private collectors prior to the realisation that this was a Roman hoard. Some of the pieces were marked with graffiti, including a cryptic sentence mentioning Lovernianus, a Romano-British name meaning 'son of a fox'. He, or his heirs, had hidden the hoard in an Appleford well.

Asthal Hoard

In 2007, a hoard of 110 gold coins was unearthed at Asthal. They had been minted between 1470 and 1526, and were of a type known as Angels and Half Angels, due to their depictions of Archangel Michael, represented as the defeater of Satan in religious iconography.

Because of these associations with beating baddies, Angels were given to the hopeful scrofula sufferers who visited Britain's monarchs to receive the royal laying-on of hands, a folkloric cure for the disease. When Angels ceased to be minted, medals known as 'touch pieces' were given instead – and these too depicted Michael and his fallen foe. By the time of the Stuarts, monarchs had become very sceptical about the tradition; but the practice continued through to the last of that family, Queen Anne, who died in 1714. It was cruelly said that the 'hands-on' of the Stuarts' successors, the little-loved Georges of Hanover, would have the opposite effect of curing.

In 2010, the Asthal Hoard was valued at £280,000 and was declared Treasure Trove. It was acquired by the Ashmolean in Oxford, and is now on display there.

Various Romano-British coins, brooches and other metal shards have been unearthed in and around Woodeaton and Beckley. Much of the treasure was discovered after the land was ploughed for the first time in the nineteenth century; but raising interest in the archaeology was not always easy. Writing in 1917, M.V. Taylor complained: 'The academic atmosphere of Oxford, sympathetic enough to the pen, has never been kindly to the use of the spade.'

The Pusey Horn

According to legend, the estate of Pusey, near Faringdon, was granted to the Puseys by King Canute in the eleventh century, after they warned him of a planned Viking attack. He sealed the contract by sending them a ceremonial drinking vessel, the Pusey Horn. This was an example of 'cornage', the transfer of land via a symbolic horn – a customary way of doing things in Anglo-Saxon England.

The Pusey Horn was donated to the Victoria & Albert Museum in London in 1938, where it can still be seen. It was originally the horn of an aurochs, the wild bovine whose name was contracted to 'ox': a highly appropriate totem object for Oxfordshire.

PLACES YOU WON'T FIND ON THE ROAD MAP...

Oxfordshire conceals a second county, **Banburyshire** – a term first coined in the early nineteenth century. It refers to the wider vicinity of Banbury, taking in small, neighbouring sections of Warwickshire and Northamptonshire. Banburyshire people seem to know what the term means, but are as slippery as eels when it comes to a formal definition.

The Baldon villages lie south-east of Oxford. A local rhyme attempts to set things straight:

Marsh Baldon, Toot Baldon, Baldon on the Green,
Little Baldon, Big Baldon, Baldon-in-between.

This would all be very helpful were it not for the fact that **Baldon on the Green, Big Baldon** and **Baldon-in-between** don't exist. An additional **Baldon St Lawrence** crops up in documents of the thirteenth century, echoing the local church dedication, and probably refers to Baldon Row, a hamlet in the Toot Baldon parish (and note that it is not mentioned in the rhyme at all). Baldon on the Green is a reference to the huge village green at Marsh Baldon. It serves as a pitch for the Baldons Cricket Club, has a pond at one side, and has a road running through the middle.

Rome lay north of Oxford University Parks, roughly in the area enclosed by modern Banbury Road, Norham Gardens and Bradmore Road. It was accessed by a track called Non Ultra and consisted of a low hill with a cave beneath, marked first with a stone cross, and later with a windmill and single house. Further north stood the gallows of Greenditch. Rome enjoyed a brief heyday as the Pleasure Gardens, but by the late nineteenth century had succumbed to housing, the main site being covered by Wycliffe Hall in 1877.

Chad is probably named after the saint of that name, although the village church opts for St Nicholas. Chad's proper name is Chadlington, known as 'the village with five ends': Brookend, Eastend, Greenend, Millend and Westend, a splendidly unimaginative piece of nomenclature. Chadlington was the birthplace of Victorian historian Sir Henry Rawlinson – not to be confused with *Sir Henry at Rawlinson End*, the character created by Vivian Stanshall for the John Peel Show in the 1970s.

The village of **Seacourt near Botley** in west Oxford was first recorded in the tenth century, when it was handed to Abingdon Abbey by King Eadwig. Legend says that it used to have twenty-four inns, to serve the needs of pilgrims visiting the nearby healing well at Binsey. But by 1439 Seacourt church had collapsed, and it was noted that only two of the village's cottages were habitable. By the time Oxford historian Anthony Wood visited in the mid-seventeenth century, Seacourt was just a few bumps in a field.

Seacourt Farm closed in 1963; however, the name survives in Botley at the Seacourt Stream, the Seacourt Bridge pub, Seacourt Tower, and Seacourt Park and Ride.

The county's other lost village is **Asterleigh**, near Kiddington. **Eaton Hastings** near Faringdon almost counts as a lost village (much of it having disappeared), but a surviving population of eighty-odd still flies the flag.

The old village of **Churchill** used to lie at the foot of Hastings Hill. Like all other settlements in late seventeenth-century England, it was assessed for Hearth Tax – a levy raised on chimneys. One baker decided to avoid paying by removing his own chimney and linking his hearth to his neighbour's chimney via a crafty hole. Unfortunately, the single chimney could not take the heat, and, on 31 July 1684, it caught fire. Twenty houses were destroyed in the conflagration, and four people roasted. In a drastic rebuilding programme, the village was relocated higher up the hill, with stone used instead of the timber and thatch of the earlier buildings. Lumps in the field around the Heritage Centre indicate where the old village used to be.

3

SAINTS AND SINNERS

GOD'S ACRE: CHURCHES AND CHURCHYARDS

Blackthorn church

Blackthorn church is not on the site originally intended. After the first day's work, the foundations were divinely upped and moved to Ambrosden overnight, and the workmen decided not to argue. This is a widespread legend – there are further examples at Checkendon and Ipsden.

St Giles' Church, Oxford

Folklore maintains that St Giles' Church in Oxford was built on an ancient temple, converted to a Convocation House in the ninth century for the prehistoric university.

Berrick Salome church

The church at Berrick Salome is an odd collaboration between brick, stone, concrete and a wooden-framed bell tower. It was upgraded in the late Victorian era by architect A. Mardon Mowbray, whose pie-in-the-sky design did not impress architecture historian Nikolaus Pevsner. His description is as clumsy as the building: 'a hideous application of all the applications of fashionable late C19 architecture to a church.' The one time of year when the church looks unequivocally lovely is Christmas Eve, when residents light candles along Church Lane.

Berrick Salome and Britwell Salome (pronounced without the 'e') are named after the Sulham family, Lords of the Manor in the thirteenth century.

Great Bourton church

The church at Great Bourton near Banbury was restructured by Victorian architect William White, who plonked a stone bell tower over the lychgate at the churchyard entrance. Only three bell towers in Britain double as lychgates.

St Mary's Church, Cuddesdon

Amongst the graves in St Mary's churchyard in Cuddesdon is a Grade II listed mediaeval cross. It was moved here in 1857 from an adjoining road, and is now in very picturesque decay, with stunted cross and shattered steps.

St James' Church, Bourton

In 2003, the poorly attended St James' Church at Bourton, on the Wiltshire border, was declared redundant by the Diocese of Oxford. The usual fate of religious edifices in these circumstances is conversion to offices, galleries, venues, private residences or restaurants. But local campaigning in Bourton managed to up the attendance and reduce the deficit, and in June 2004 the sentence of spiritual death was rescinded.

St Margaret's Church, Little Faringdon

All churches have dedications – that is, a saint after whom they are named. Sometimes the only trace of a lost church is a saint's name in written records. It is highly unusual for a dedication to be unknown – but this is the case at Little Faringdon, on the Gloucestershire border near Lechlade. Investigations revealed no saint, and so in 2000 the church authorities dedicated it to St Margaret of England, a twelfth-century Cistercian nun and a relative of Thomas Becket of Canterbury. The relevance lies in the Cistercian connection: Little Faringdon was owned by the Cistercian monks of Beaulieu Abbey before the Dissolution of the Monasteries.

St James' Church, Bix

Bix Bottom is an area of land north of the village of Bix, near Henley. It contains Warburg Nature Reserve and the ruins of St James' Church, a Norman foundation abandoned in 1874 when someone had the bright idea of building a new St James in Bix itself. The ruin was included as a location in the low-budget 1971 Hammer Horror *Blood on Satan's Claw*.

Black Bourton church

In 1866, Canon James Lupton, vicar of Black Bourton, discovered eleventh-century paintings on the walls of his church. The scenes from the New Testament include Christ's baptism by John the Baptist, with an invigilating angel; cheerily waving portraits of Saints Peter and Paul; and St Stephen being stoned by a wild-haired executioner. But, while Lupton was away in London, the church curate slapped whitewash over the paintings. The outraged vicar wrote to the curate's landlords, Christ Church College, condemning the vandalism – but the College failed to intervene. Ironically, the curate's whitewash

South Newington.

preserved the paintings, which were uncovered again with much care and a greater sense of preservation in 1932.

St Mary's Church, Chalgrove

Several other Oxfordshire churches have mediaeval wall paintings. The fourteenth-century ones at St Mary's in Chalgrove, preserved by the application of lime wash during the Reformation under Henry VIII, were uncovered in 1858. Although faded, the paintings have given St Mary's a Grade I listing.

South Newington church

South Newington has fragments of fourteenth and fifteenth-century paintings, including an image of Christ entering Jerusalem on a tiny donkey. It is painted with such artlessness that it steals the show.

Church of St Peter and St Paul, Checkendon

Checkendon Church of St Peter and St Paul has thirteenth-century paintings, again uncovered by the renovating Victorians and over-enthusiastically 'restored'. More recently, a painting featuring a knight on a horse was discovered behind the organ, and this has been gently restored rather than reinvented.

Dorchester-on-Thames and Horley churches

Dorchester-on-Thames church has frescos dating from 1340, along with nineteenth-century additions to the artwork. Horley's contribution to the genre is a fifteenth-century St Zita. Like St Anthony, she can be invoked in the search for lost keys, one of which she is carrying in the faded painting.

Depictions of St Christopher

St Christopher was a popular subject for mediaeval Oxfordshire church painters – his association with water allowing them to trawl their imaginations. At Bloxham, for example, there is an attendant mermaid; at Horley there is a fisherman, a fish and a leaping sturgeon; at Combe there is an otter; and at Woodeaton, which wins first prize, the saint is in the company of a human-headed octopus.

Horley's Christopher includes a rhyming-couplet conversation with Jesus, who in legend was carried across a river by the saint. Christopher comments that Christ is the heaviest thing he has ever borne. Jesus does not take offence, pointing out: 'Yey, I be hevy no wonder ys for I am yey kynge of blys.'

The county has many other Christopher depictions, including a very faded image at Dorchester-on-Thames, where the watery saint stands more than 4m high.

Kencot church

Kencot church has a twelfth-century relief carving of the centaur Sagittarius, firing arrows at a monstrous head. It may symbolise Christ's Harrowing of Hell. This important moment in mythology occurred between the Crucifixion and the Resurrection, when Jesus went to Hell and freed the souls of the pre-Christians, from Adam and Eve onwards, who had been awaiting the Salvation.

Sagittarius was the emblem of Etienne de Blois, aka King Stephen, who reigned at the time the church was built. This suggests an alternative symbolism; however, Kencot belonged to the d'Oilly family, who were fierce opponents of Stephen and loyal to his cousin and rival, the Empress Matilda (daughter of Henry I, mother of Henry II), so the unique carving remains enigmatic.

Oxford churchyards

When an 1843 commission revealed that Oxford's burial grounds were full, a new general city cemetery was mooted. The clergy, fiercely loyal to their own little plots of anciently consecrated ground, refused to co-operate.

By 1855 the full churchyards were even fuller, in spite of new land having been consecrated in Osney, Jericho and Holywell, and it was announced that burials must cease in all the parish churchyards. The only people who could now be interred were those who owned family plots and vaults. There was no additional space in Catholic, Baptist,

Wesleyan or Congregational graveyards, nor in the city workhouse, the Radcliffe Infirmary or the castle gaol.

In 1878, east Oxford gained the St Mary and St John churchyard, but the rest of the city had to cope with corpse chaos until 1889–90, when municipal cemeteries at Rose Hill, Wolvercote and Botley were opened. Headington was co-opted in when the former village became an Oxford suburb in 1928, and its crematorium went up in smoke in 1939.

ABBEYS AND PRIORIES

Dorchester

In AD 634, the Thames Valley was devoutly pagan. The man who put a stop to all this was Birinus, sent over by Pope Honorius I to carry out mass conversions. Local King Cynegils was a sympathiser, and he granted Birinus land at Dorchester-on-Thames, which became the administrative centre of the Diocese of Dorchester, covering most of Wessex and Mercia (i.e. most of the South and the Midlands). Birinus' relics at Dorchester were a major pilgrim attraction in the Middle Ages, although the bones interred here were almost certainly not those of the saint.

Dorchester housed Augustinian friars after the twelfth century, but they were booted out following the Reformation. The abbey church survived, and contains treasures a-plenty. These include a 'Tree of Jesse', its stone branches snaking up a window; the effigy of an unknown knight, limbs twisted and right arm reaching for his sword as though he has just fallen in battle; and some surprising faces in the building's gargoyle menagerie, including American Edith Stedman, who was instrumental in restoring the church in the 1960s, and whose efforts won her an honorary OBE.

Abingdon Abbey

Abingdon Abbey was established in 675 by West Saxon King Cissa, as a residence for twelve Benedictine monks. It was soon raking in lands and money, until the Danish Vikings torched the lot in the late ninth century. King Alfred subsequently defeated the Danes, offering to return the abbey to the monks if they showed their appreciation; but, when they failed to deliver sufficient booty, Alfred took back with one hand what he had given with the other – a popular political trick ever since – moving the abbey's vast acres into his own real estate portfolio and handing it out to his own cronies.

The monastery was re-established under King Edgar in the mid-tenth century, under the guidance of monastic reformer Ethelwold, who went on to become Bishop of Winchester and a saint. His feast day is 1 August, although he was never officially canonised. The basis of his saintdom is a cult established two years after his death, when Aelfric of Wallingford claimed to have been cured of blindness at his tomb. Abingdon Abbey dusted down an arm and a leg of the saint to feed the relic-hungry pilgrims, and the unofficial sanctity has been in place ever since.

There is an alternative story, though. According to the 1164 *History of the Church of Abingdon*, a fifth-century British prince called Aben was one of the fleet-footed few who escaped the knives of Saxon warlord Hengist, who had tricked the British aristocracy into attending a feast at Stonehenge, during which most of them were stabbed to death. Retiring from political life, Aben established a hermitage at 'Abendon Hill', and in AD 675, this site, somewhere near Cumnor, was chosen by local Prince Hean as the location of a new religious institution.

Hean's church on Abendon Hill had teething problems, however. Everything he built fell down overnight. Just as Hean was thinking of giving up, a hermit from Cumnor Wood told him he had seen, in a vision, a group of men relocating all Hean's handiwork from Abendon Hill to a new site. It was God's will to have the church built down in the river valley, he said. Hean went to investigate and discovered foundations marked out by furrows in the earth. Ignoring the tongue-twister, he abandoned Abendon and built an abbey at Abingdon.

The purpose of this legend was to give the religious institution the earliest possible foundation date. The earlier the abbey, the more chance of patronage, pilgrims and cash – and the more chance of claiming back lands taken away during the recent civil wars and political upheavals. That was the *real* point of the book.

A few bits of the Abingdon Abbey can still be seen, including a timber-framed long gallery, the abbey exchequer, the bakehouse, a heavily restored gateway, a hostel for pilgrims, and the twelfth-century Church of St Nicholas.

St Frideswide's Priory
St Frideswide is Oxford's patron saint. An eighth-century princess, she became a nun at the convent built by her father, King Didan, in what later became Oxford. But her beauty bewitched another regional

king, Algar. He threatened to enslave her in a brothel if she refused to marry him.

The men sent to apprehend Frideswide were struck blind by a Divine bolt from the blue, allowing Frideswide to escape. Guided by an angel, she sailed down the Thames to Bampton, where she took shelter in an abandoned swineherd's hut. Algar tracked her down, and was on the verge of violence when he too was struck blind.

Frideswide stayed in hiding for three years after this, performing miracles that boosted her holy reputation. She lived briefly in a self-built oratory near Binsey, before returning to the convent. She forgave Algar and cured his blindness, after which he retired, humble and holy.

Frideswide's nunnery was burnt down during a massacre of resident Danes in 1002, but in 1122 St Frideswide's Priory was built on the same spot. It was dissolved and claimed by Cardinal Wolsey in 1524, who made it part of the University: Cardinal College. His hubris was repaid when he fell from favour in 1530; Henry VIII confiscated and refounded the institution as Christ Church College, and the old priory church became Christ Church Cathedral.

The latter edifice is unique in being not just a former monastic church, but at the same time the chapel of a College and a city diocese cathedral.

Christ Church Cathedral.

Osney Abbey

Edith, wife of Robert d'Oilly and later a
saint, was persuaded to found Osney
Abbey in Oxford after an encounter
with magpies in 1129. She was walking
by the Thames, when, according to
1660s' chronicler Anthony Wood,
she saw 'a great company of pyes
gathered together on a tree, making
a hideous noise with their chattering'.
They were there the following day, and
the next, 'seeming as 'twere to direct
their chatterings to her'.

Osney Abbey.

Edith consulted Radulphus, a monk of Oxford's St Frideswide's,
for advice. After witnessing the magpies, he declared: 'These are no
pyes, but so many poor souls in purgatory that do begg and make all
this complaint for succour and relief.' Edith determined to bring this
black and white matter to a close, founding the abbey 'near or upon
the place where these pyes chattered'. Radulphus, whom Wood terms
'the wiliest pye of them all', became its first prior.

Today, nothing remains of the well and truly dissolved abbey – except
part of its later mill building, recently redeveloped as flats.

Rewley Abbey

Rewley Abbey in Oxford was established around 1280 as a college
for Cistercian monks. Abbot Nicholas Austen, seeing the fatal
storm of the Dissolution approaching in 1536, offered Henry VIII's
henchman, Thomas Cromwell, £100 to save the monastery and allow
it to continue as a University College. Cromwell, as ever, had his eye
on the establishment's treasure, and refused the bribe. Austen was
given a pension and very wisely left town, moving to Cambridge to
end his life in academia.

Stanton Harcourt and Bicester

The church at Stanton Harcourt contains remnants of the shrine of
St Edburga, or Eadburgh (died AD 650). The shrine and saint's relics
were originally housed in Bicester Priory, but the latter were moved to
a shrine at Flanders in 1500. Edburga herself was an Aylesbury nun,
her father being the warrior King Penda of Mercia. Her sisters Edith
and Cuneburga also became saints, as did their niece Osith. Their
pagan father must have been furious.

Modern Bicester's main church is St Edburga's, and the care home St Edburg's House occupies the site of the old priory church.

Godstow Nunnery

Godstow Nunnery was founded in 1133 by visionary Ediva, or Edith, who had literally seen the light – shining from Heaven and marking the place of imminent construction. It is famous for its associations with Fair Rosamund (*see* p.92). Poignant ruins still stand at Godstow, near Oxford.

Holy Trinity Monastery

Benedictine nuns conquer cyberspace ... In 2004, Holy Trinity Monastery at East Hendred near Wantage opened: the first new Benedictine establishment for fifty years. Its first members were nuns from Stanbrook Abbey in Worcester. But this is no backward-looking institution. The nuns fund the monastery via book and web design, audio books, and a website that includes a 'Virtual Retreat', designed by in-house webmaster DigitalNun, the monastery's prioress.

DigitalNun is attempting to create an online monastic community, and there is even a version of the website for mobile devices. As it says on their unorthodox pages:

> The internet is a great way of making monastic life more accessible without destroying the peace and recollection of the cloister ... We know many people are time-poor, hence our development of online retreats to allow a little monastic space in the midst of daily activity.

The remains of Godstow Nunnery.

CATHOLIC TASTES

Nicholas Breakspear

It is well known in Oxford that University alumnus Nicholas Breakspear (1100–59) was the first recorded parish priest of Binsey near the city, and that he later went on to become Adrian IV – first, and so far only, English Pope. The Oxfordshire connection is underlined by the fact that the surname exists locally in historical records, and continues with Brakspear Brewery at Henley-on-Thames.

However, evidence for the English Pope's Oxfordshire incumbency is elusive, to put it mildly. He appears to have been born in St Albans, Hertfordshire, and probably studied at Oxford, but left the country to pursue his vocation abroad at an early age. The confusion has probably arisen from Binsey records listing an early parish priest called Breakspear. The rest is the usual stew of darkness, leaps of faith and apocrypha.

The Binsey legend traces back to an unsubstantiated statement in the journal *Notes & Queries* in 1879, and was perpetuated by the classic *Oxford* by Jan (formerly James) Morris in 1965.

The Eyston family

The Eyston family have lived at Hendred House in East Hendred since the fifteenth century. They survived in spite of taking the dangerous path of being recusants – that is, remaining Catholic when the rest of the country went Protestant, a decision that resulted in torture and death for many. Hendred House's private chapel of St Amand and St John the Baptist has been in continuous use as a Catholic church since it was first built in the thirteenth century.

East Hendred's parish church has a sixteenth-century clock, built by John Seymour of Wantage, that plays *Angel's Hymn* by composer Orlando Gibbons every three hours – to leaven the bread of its more conventional repertoire of strikes and chimes. Prime Minister David Cameron was married in the church in 1996, five years before becoming MP for Witney.

Catholic sanctuaries

Recusants were tucked away in other quiet corners of Oxfordshire too. On the Buckinghamshire border at Godington, the Catholics outnumbered the Protestants – even in the mid-eighteenth century. They gathered at the chapel of the local Fermor family in Tusmore Park, and later in a converted loft at the moat house beside the parish church, ministered by a priest from Hethe. At Somerton, near Bicester, it was said that forty-seven Roman Catholics attended monthly Mass at the manor house chapel during 1738. They were part of the community, and remained respectful to the Church of England vicar and his flock – so much so that a blind eye was turned, in spite of the fact that Catholic congregations were illegal. Shirburn Castle was another recusant bolt-hole.

In spite of these sanctuaries, recusants were in a precarious position until the Roman Catholic Relief Act of 1791, which decriminalised the religion.

Edmund Campion

In 1581 Edmund Campion, a leading recusant, was unearthed in hidden chambers at Lyford Grange Manor in Lyford, by the religious bloodhounds of Elizabeth II. Campion had fled here from another recusant stronghold at Stonor Park. The Grange was the home of Francis Yate, who housed other Catholics, including a troop of Bridgettine nuns.

Campion was driven through Oxford, where he was greeted by some as a hero. He was a Fellow of St John's College, and had led a debate in front of Elizabeth in happier times. She had, indeed, voiced her high regard for the man, who had also managed to win favour with the previous queen, the Catholic Mary I. This religious spin came to an end when Campion decided to come down from the fence as a Jesuit priest preaching in secret at Stonor; the former affections of Elizabeth and the University were not enough to save him. He was later tortured, hanged, drawn and quartered.

Edmund Campion and the two priests arrested with him at Lyford – Thomas Ford and John Colleton – are commemorated annually with a church Mass at Lyford. In 1970, Campion's long spiritual journey was complete when he was made a saint by the Roman Catholic Church. Thomas Ford got there earlier, sanctified in 1889.

In spite of its associations with Campion, the thirteenth-century chapel in Stonor Park somehow weathered the storm, and, like the one at East Hendred, has retained an uninterrupted Catholic service.

The Prebendal

The building known as the Prebendal in Thame was built in the thirteenth century as a 'prebend' – the residence of the prebendary, a Church official who received tithes and income from the parish. After the Reformation, the Prebendal was abandoned (in 1547) and was a ruin until renovated in 1836.

In the early twentieth century the property was purchased by Colonel Grisewood, who brought Catholic services back to the chapel in the Prebendal's grounds. But the family's religious leanings were not universally welcome. Grisewood's son Harman (BBC Executive, announcer and actor) recalled how he and his brother were once taken out in their prams by a nanny and nursemaid, and were stoned by irate villagers as they approached the town's Anglican church.

If things ever turn ugly again at the Prebendal, there is an escape route. Legend speaks of a secret tunnel that runs from the house to the site of Notley Abbey, on the banks of the River Thame near Long Crendon.

The Caversham shrine

The highly popular shrine of Our Lady at Caversham used to contain a silver-plated statue of the Blessed Virgin Mary. The Mary-onette was dressed in clothes, cap, wig, and a crown made from 20lb of gold left in the 1439 will of Isabella Beauchamp, Countess of Warwick. This was just the sort of thing that stood no chance of surviving the anti-idolatry Reformation in the sixteenth century.

Henry's icon-busting henchman, Dr John London, descended on the Caversham shrine in 1538, destroying what he described as 'many pretty relics'. It was not until 1958 that the shrine, refitted and re-consecrated, reopened to pilgrims.

John Henry Newman

John Henry Newman was one of the leaders of the 1830s' Oxford Movement – a religious swing from Low Church Anglicanism to the older, ritual practices of Catholicism. The movement had its origins at Oxford University and was headline-grabbing stuff at the time. Newman took his Anglo-Catholic philosophy to its natural extreme, becoming a Catholic cardinal in 1845. He died in 1890, a highly respected academic, author and member of the Catholic intellectual elite. Memory of the man still looms large at his base in Littlemore, home of Newman College.

In 2008, it was decided that his remains should be translated to a shrine at Birmingham Oratory. Pope Benedict XVI bestowed beatification on Newman in 2010, declaring him to be safely installed in Heaven and available for answering prayers. By 2019, it was confirmed that Newman had performed the requisite miracles needed for sainthood.

However, that 2008 attempt to translate the man's relics to the shrine hit a bizarre and insurmountable problem. When the coffin was opened, there were no bones inside. It was postulated that they had rotted completely in the damp ground, but forensic experts declared this highly unlikely and the mystery remains unsolved. Having no relics is a bit of a setback, but that did not prevent Newman being canonised on 13 October 2019 by Pope Francis. The UK's official representative at the ceremony in St. Peter's Square was Prince Charles. St John Henry Newman's feast day is 9 October, the date of his conversion to Catholicism.

CHURCHMEN AND CHURCH-GOERS

Cuddesdon
The Bishop of Oxford's chief residence used to be Cuddesdon Palace. The original building was knocked down by Royalists in the English Civil War, just ten years after its erection, to prevent the advancing Parliamentarian forces from using it during the forthcoming Siege of Oxford. Its 1679 replacement burnt down in the 1960s, with just a chapel escaping ruin.

Cuddesdon College was founded near the site in 1854, and today, as Ripon College Cuddesdon, it still trains Anglican clergy. Former Archbishop of Canterbury Robert Runcie, one-time vicar in the village, took the title Baron Runcie of Cuddesdon. These deep-rooted connections have given the site the local tag Holy Hill.

Communion
It is a popular belief that, prior to the twentieth century, everyone attended church and received communion. In reality, the usual minimum requirement in Oxfordshire was three communions a year, sometimes just one. Even so, in 1619 the churchwardens of Sutton stated that half the parish were failing to meet this low benchmark. The parish of Cropredy declared that it gave communion three times a year as required, but was unsure how many of the population actually took it.

Catechism
It is another popular myth that people were better acquainted with the Bible in 'the old days'. In the seventeenth century, parishioners were required to memorise a bare minimum, as set out in Edward Fenton's 'So Shorte a Catechisme, That Whosoever Cannot, or Wil Not Learne, Are Not in Any Wise to be Admitted to the Lords

Supper'. But many failed to study. In 1584, Richard Turland, unable to recite this catechism, was refused communion at Bloxham. His answer to this dilemma was to go to neighbouring King's Sutton and get a crafty communion there.

Aston Tirrold

Aston Tirrold was an early hotbed of religious dissent and unconformity. Between 1661 and 1665, a series of Acts known as the Clarendon Code (after Charles II's Lord Chancellor Edward Hyde, Earl of Clarendon) had prescribed all the texts and rituals required for practicing Anglican clergy. Many ministers refused to fall in line, and at least 2,000 were kicked out of the Church of England, many Oxfordshire men amongst them. They never looked back.

A Presbyterian community was established at Aston Tirrold soon after 1662. The religious freedom this offered was offset by the fact that adherents could not hold any public office, occupy an official religious edifice, or come within 5 miles of their former churches or of any towns with a Corporation – they suffered the Anglican equivalent of an excommunication.

The leading local dissenters were Thomas Cheesman, former vicar of East Garston in Berkshire, and Richard Comyns, erstwhile incumbent of Cholsey. They happily did without churches, preaching to their followers in barns and open spaces. They swayed hundreds to their way of thinking via the Society of Dissenters, founded at Aston Tirrold in the late 1660s.

Banbury

Puritanism found its most extreme outlet in Banbury, spurred on by the parliamentary ranting of its MP, Sir Anthony Cope. He had pulled down the Maypole at Neithrop, after winning a court case following a Puritan-versus-Mayday revellers' riot in 1589. It was believed that all images relating to Christianity were idolatrous vestiges of Catholicism and paganism. With all of the town's churches stripped to a pleasing grey, the only villains left were Banbury's crosses.

Chief target was the fifteenth-century **High Cross** or **Market Cross**, in Cornhill off the Market Place. Pretty and innocuous to many, it was a symbol of idolatry to others; Puritans, led by William Knight, Richard Wheatley, Thomas Wheatley and Henry Shewell, toppled it in 1600. At the inquest that followed, anti-Puritan observer Matthew Knight said he had seen the men, in a company of more than 150, hack at the cross with axes:

William Knight with a great voice did encourage and animate the said workmen saying, 'Come let us down with it and down with it quickly', and presently the spire of the said high cross did fall to the ground to the great discontentment of many that were present. The said Shewell cried out, 'God be thanked, their god Dagon is fallen down to the ground!'

The town's **Bread Cross**, at the corner of High Street and Butcher's Row, suffered the same fate. It had been a very practical structure, with a slate roof offering shelter for the bread and meat stalls that used to trade there. A Good Friday bread dole was annually handed out here too.

A third structure, the **White Cross** – a boundary cross situated at what is now the corner of West Bar Street and Beargarden Road – seems to have survived the vandalism.

The modern Banbury Cross, dominating the crossroads in the centre of the town, was erected in 1859 to mark the marriage of Queen Victoria's eldest daughter, Victoria Adelaide Mary Louisa, to Friedrich Wilhelm of Prussia.

John Wesley

John Wesley visited Thame to preach Methodism in the 1780s. His congregation met on the top floor of a cottage on a site now occupied by Coral's bookmakers (which J.W. would most certainly not have approved of). The numbers were so great that the floor collapsed, spilling the congregation to the room below. It was a powerful symbol of the downward direction they might take in the afterlife.

Many of Thame's cottages were in poor repair back then, as the town was occupied predominantly by agricultural labourers on extremely low pay. The fact that the workhouse (currently part of Oxford & Cherwell Valley College) was the biggest building in town speaks volumes.

John White

One of the non-conformist ministers responsible for establishing the colony at Massachusetts in New England was John White. He was born at Stanton St John, near Oxford, in 1575. Towards the end of his life, he was made warden of New College (a post formerly held by his uncle), but, due to ill health, he never actually ventured into the city to take up the post. He never visited America either, but was responsible for negotiating the charter for the Massachusetts Bay

New College.

Company that made it all possible. His son, another John, became a successful merchant in the New England town of Boston.

Tetsworth – 'Botany Bay'

Tetsworth acquired a reputation for religious non-conformity, avoiding the usual Anglican parson-squire domination, and thriving as a so-called 'open village' in which there was a relatively large amount of freedom to do, say and go where you pleased. This earned it the nickname Botany Bay, after the supposedly lawless prison colony-cum-settlement in New South Wales, Australia.

4

THE ART OF BEING FAMOUS

DIVERSE ROADS TO FAME

Timothy Tyrell

Timothy Tyrell was Master of the Buckhounds to King James I's eldest son Prince Henry in the early seventeenth century. After a hunt in Shotover Forest, Timothy held the head of a buck so that the Prince could kill it; but, in cutting its throat, Henry's blade slipped, wounding Tyrell's hand so badly that he was permanently maimed. In compensation he received a grant, in 1613, of lands at Shotover, and he was knighted there in 1624. Henry did less well, dying in 1612, aged eighteen.

Reverend Richard Stone

Wadham College Fellow, Revd Richard Stone (1702–68), is the spiritual father of aspirin. His investigations into the analgesic effects of willow bark paved the way for the later drug, and a Blue Plaque on West Street in his hometown of Chipping Norton commemorates this.

Having chewed the bark and noted its effects, Stone's initial conclusions were wide of the mark. He believed that aches and pains known as 'agues' originated in damp places associated with willows. He maintained that 'remedies lie not far from their causes', hence his experimentation with the bark. He was not being altogether innovative, however: the pain-killing properties of this family of plants were known to Hippocrates in 400 BC.

In his subsequent experiments, Stone effectively discovered the active ingredient – salicylic acid – announcing his breakthrough in 1763. It was a less corrosive compound of the acid that was eventually used to produce modern aspirin, registered as a trade name by German company A.G. Bayer in 1899.

Alfred White

Alfred White established his bell-hanging business after befriending bell-caster Thomas Mears, who was fitting six new bells at Appleton church. Trading as A.White & Sons, he was soon working on churches and cathedrals nationwide. When Alfred died, his son Frederick took over the a-pealing business with even greater zeal, installing massive oak bell frames at Christ Church, Merton and Magdalen Colleges in Oxford. He also designed and manufactured clock-chime mechanisms.

In 1969 the company became Whites of Appleton, and in 1985 Frederick White's old workshop was superseded by a modern factory. The company is still thriving, and is now the oldest continuously trading bell-hanging company in the country.

A bell fund appeal at Cropredy near Banbury raised enough money to cast two new bells in 2006, hung by Whites of Appleton. They were in place and rededicated on 17 February 2008. One is called St Mary, inscribed 'Cropredy villagers gave me', and the other is the Fairport Convention Festival Bell. This is in recognition of the band Fairport Convention, who played a benefit concert for the appeal, and whose annual music festival has been staged at Cropredy since 1980.

Jethro Tull

Agricultural pioneer Jethro Tull of Crowmarsh Gifford invented the horse-drawn seed drill in 1701. His achievement is commemorated on a Blue Plaque at his cottage on the village's main road. The seed drill was one of the labour- and time-saving innovations at the heart of the Agricultural Revolution; Tull followed the invention with a horse-drawn hoe, intended as a means of phasing out the use of oxen.

Tull's interest in a more intensive, scientific approach to farming came after a heart condition had led him to visit Europe in search of a decent doctor. He studied agricultural practices en route, convinced that, as with his own health problems, it was not practical or desirable to leave everything to the whims of nature.

Ironically, given this secular approach to the subject, it was in church that Tull had his brilliant idea. He was looking at the church organ pipes with their holes and stops, and realised that this was the way forward with seed drills: boxes of seed with several drilled pipes through which the grains were delivered when the device was pulled.

And yes, the rock band Jethro Tull was named after him. Its founder Ian Anderson has, appropriately enough, spent much of his life as a farmer.

William Buckland

William Buckland was Oxford's first lecturer in Geology, and he and his son Frank were two of the most colourful characters ever produced by the University. Both kept houses that doubled as menageries, and their knowledge of all things animal – including how edible the various species were – was enormous. Buckland senior used to claim that he had eaten has way through the whole of animal creation: at first he thought the mole was the nastiest thing he had ever tasted, but later decided that blue-bottles were worse.

William Tuckwell, writing about the Bucklands, recalls:

> Frank used to tell of their visit ... to a foreign cathedral, where was exhibited a martyr's blood-dark spots on the pavement ever fresh and ineradicable. The professor dropped on the pavement and touched the stain with his tongue. 'I can tell you what it is; it is bat's urine!'

This was not his only episode of myth-debunking. During a visit to the shrine of St Rosalia in Palermo, Sicily, he asked to see the famous bones of the saint:

> [The shrine] was opened by the priests, and the relics of the saint were shown ... 'They are the bones of a goat', he cried out, 'not of a woman'; and the sanctuary doors were abruptly closed.

This original Mad Professor died on 24 August 1856, aged seventy-three, and is buried in Islip at a spot pre-chosen by him in the village churchyard.

James Sadler

The second balloonist, and the first Englishman, to take off from England was James Sadler. Inspired by the ascent of Vincent Lunardi at Moorfields in London less than a month previously, on 4 October 1784 Sadler took off from Oxford's Christ Church Meadow, touching down 6 miles later at Woodeaton. He had reached a maximum height of 1,100m (3,600ft) during the journey. In the following year, he made it as far as Aylesbury.

Sadler's third ride in the balloon took place in May 1785, and upon landing (near Pontefract in Yorkshire, having taken off from a garden on what was later called Balloon Street in Manchester), he was dragged for 2 miles by the brake-free balloon. In spite of this he remained a regular aeronaut, narrowly escaping drowning on a couple of occasions when his vehicle plunged into water. It was the death of his youngest son, Windham, in a ballooning accident in 1824 that finally deflated his spirits. He died in 1828 aged seventy-five.

Martyrs' Memorial

George Gilbert Scott's Martyrs' Memorial on St Giles' in Oxford commemorates three men burned at the stake by Mary I. Archbishops Cranmer, Latimer and Ridley died for the principles of the Protestant Reformation, which were under threat in 1830s' Oxford. Not only was Catholic emancipation looking inevitable, but all manner of Low Church alternatives to the Church of England were muddying the Orthodox waters too. The memorial's inscription mentions 'the sacred truths which they [the martyrs] had affirmed and maintained against the errors of the Church of Rome'.

Some of the project's critics were scathing. A.W.N. Pugin, a giant in architecture and father of the Victorian Gothic revival, issued a pamphlet on the subject. He spoke of the 'atrocities' committed by the so-called martyrs under their own anti-Catholic tenure, and described the proposed memorial as a puny construction in a city 'which owes its very existence to Catholic piety'.

The project went ahead regardless, in spite of shortfalls in funding due to subscribers who had not coughed up. The project committee had to borrow £250 from the parish of St Mary Magdalen (of which £200 is still outstanding). The committee had cannily ensured that their personal liability should not exceed £10 per member, a sum later reduced to £5. The parish had to stump up even more, paying for the martyrs-related fixtures and alterations in the neighbouring church. £9,333 16s 4½d was the final cost of the folly, and Gilbert Scott was magnanimous enough to forgo part of his fee due to lack of funds.

The memorial, completed in 1843, has since become a landmark in the city, its anti-Catholic sentiments largely forgotten. It is also the object of a traditional practical joke, in which visitors and newcomers to the city are told that the spire-like monument is actually the top of a subterranean church.

Joseph Vallard

Joseph Vallard was arrested at St Giles' Fair in Oxford, 1888. Apprehended in his rags, he told police that his name was Jesus Devilheart, Marquis of Anjou, Commander of the Forces in Heaven and Earth, Lord Mayor of London and Mayor of Oxford, a descendant of Richard Coeur de Lion and the Plantagenets, 'and thus from William the Conqueror, and also from Napoleon the First'.

He was found not guilty of the charge of being 'a rogue and vagabond', but was kept in gaol for a week so that his mental state could be examined.

Frank Lascelle

Frank Lascelle of Sibford Gower was known as 'The Man Who Staged the Empire'. He was a pioneer of pageants – cast-heavy spectaculars which gained popularity in the early twentieth century. Lascelle choreographed huge numbers of people in his extravaganzas. The first production was the 'Oxford Historical' in 1907, receiving the public thumbs-up in spite of opposition from Oxford University (which baulked at the huge numbers involved) and in spite of an accompanying student riot that harked back to the Town versus Gown brawls of bygone years.

Prestige followed, and in 1908 Lascelle put together a pageant in Quebec for the Tercentenary of Canada, involving hundreds of Iroquois Indians, who made him an honorary Chief, re-naming him Tehonikonraka, 'man of infinite resource'. Similar honours were bestowed in South Africa when his cast of thousands graced the Union Parliament in Cape Town: he was named Chief Rakalello of the Basutos tribe, 'father of wonderful thoughts'.

The scale grew ever bigger – 15,000 at the Pageant of London, 300,000 at the Coronation Durbar Pageant in Calcutta. Whenever an Empire theme was mooted for a celebration, Lascelle was wheeled out as Master of the Pageant. He died in 1934.

Jerome K. Jerome and Peter Pan

In *Three Men in a Boat*, author Jerome K. Jerome describes the pool behind the lock at Sandford-on-Thames near Henley as 'a very good place to drown yourself'. This was a cynical reference to the spot's long history of drownings, a consequence of some surprisingly strong currents and eddies. An obelisk by the river records the deaths of six Christ Church students, and seems to have been erected in expectation of disaster: the installation of the stone itself predates the earliest of these deaths (1843) by more than twenty years.

One of the students drowned was, shockingly, Peter Pan. Michael Llewelyn Davies perished here in 1921 after an ill-advised plunge. He was the adopted son of author J.M. Barrie, and the model for Peter Pan.

Jerome K. Jerome spent the last years of his life at Ewelme near Wallingford, and his ashes were buried there, at St Mary's churchyard, in 1927.

William Archibald Spooner

The master of metathesis (the switching of consonants or syllables in a phrase or sentence) was New College warden William Archibald Spooner (1844–1940), reluctant source of the word 'Spoonerism'. His tips of the slung include, 'The Lord is a shoving leopard...'; 'let us glaze our rasses to the queer old Dean'; 'a well boiled icicle'; 'a half warmed fish'; and 'You have hissed all my mystery lectures. You have tasted a whole worm. Please leave Oxford on the next town drain.' Sadly, they all appear to be apocryphal: Spooner himself said that the phrase 'Kinquering Congs their titles take' was his only genuine 'Spoonerism'.

Margaret Papakura

Oddington church, on the edge of Otmoor, has an unusual feature at its west side: a statue of Mary and Jesus (*a pietà*) decorated with brightly gurning Māori totems. This is a memorial to Māori servicemen who took part in the First World War. It was installed by Margaret Papakura (aka Makereti), a resident of mixed Māori-British parentage who settled in the village. She took part in the war effort by assisting recuperating soldiers from New Zealand, and was buried in Oddington church. The grave is a place of pilgrimage for New Zealanders keen to acknowledge her contribution to Māori culture, and items from her Kiwi cultural collection are kept at the Pitt Rivers Museum in Oxford.

Part of this collection, some tattooed Māori heads, was removed in 1987 after a quiet word from a visiting Māori dignitary. Amazonian decapitees are still on display, however, in spite of ethical concerns, looking like the Dorian Gray images of Victorian porcelain dolls.

Sir Tim Berners-Lee

Sir Tim Berners-Lee (born 1955) studied at Queen's College, Oxford, gaining a First in Physics. He went on to change the entire world, effectively inventing the World Wide Web. Commenting on this achievement, he said with accustomed modesty: 'I just had to take the hypertext idea and connect it to the Transmission Control Protocol and domain name system ideas and – ta-da! – the World Wide Web.'

Nick Leeson

The 1720 Ardington House, near Ardington, is the private residence of the Baring family. Originally wool merchants from Exeter, they founded the merchant bank Barings in 1762. Unfortunately, the bank's biggest claim to fame is its publicity-drenched collapse in 1995. It was by then London's oldest merchant bank, with a venerable reputation scuppered by employee Nick Leeson, who famously lost £827 million after speculative investing in futures contracts in Singapore. The devastating Kobe earthquake was the unlikely cause of Leeson's, and Barings', downfall. It struck in January 1995, claiming nearly 6,500 lives, and sending the Asian markets into a downward spin.

With Leeson later in prison, Barings was eventually sold to a Dutch bank for the nominal sum of £1. A jacket reputedly worn by Leeson whilst trading during the infamous Singapore years was later sold for £21,000, such is the weird way of the world.

LITERARY FAME

So many famous writers and artists, from Geoffrey Chaucer to Philip Pullman, have passed through Oxford University that it would take this entire book just to list them all. Suffice to say that fans of Philip Sidney, Samuel Johnson, Richard Hakluyt, W.H. Auden, Louis MacNeice, Angus Wilson, Nathaniel Hawthorne, Thomas Hughes, Edward Thomas, Alan Bennett, Dr Seuss (T.S. Geisel), John le Carré, Jeanette Winterson and countless others, will find suitable places of pilgrimage in Oxford.

Ben Jonson

On his way from London to Stratford-upon-Avon, paying social calls to his retired friend William Shakespeare, playwright Ben Jonson regularly stopped for beer at Weston-on-the-Green. The thatched pub is now known as the Ben Jonson, and why bother arguing with such a simple, satisfying, hard-to-disprove legend?

The friendship is thought to have been genuine enough. Shakespeare was on the cast list in Jonson's second play, *Every Man in his Humour*, when it was performed in 1598 by the Lord Chamberlain's men at London's Globe Theatre.

William D'Avenant

Dramatist William D'Avenant was born in Oxford, where his father John kept the Crown Inn, off Cornmarket. It is said to be the house where D'Avenant's friend William Shakespeare wrote *A Winter's Tale*. Scandalmongers have even claimed that young D'Avenant was the Bard's love child.

George Withers

Worst Oxfordshire poem ever? Possibly this, from George Withers, 1620, writing of the Thameside spot called Medley (marked by Medley – aka Rainbow – Bridge) near Binsey:

> In summer time to Medley my love and I would go,
> The boatmen there stood ready, my love and I to row:
> For cream there would we call, for cakes and prunes too,
> But now alas she's left me, Falero, lero, loo.

John Milton

The poet John Milton, of *Paradise Lost* fame, was unlucky in love. His first marriage took place at Forest Hill in 1640, but the young bride, Mary Powell, 'being not well pleas'd with his reserv'd manner of life, within a few days left him, and went back into the Country with her Mother', according to a biographical account. She succumbed to his charms four years later, blaming her mother's snobbery for the curtailed nuptial bliss. But it was too late: the flames of love had died, and Milton wished to rekindle elsewhere. He gained a divorce and went blind. The two events are not related.

Milton is commemorated in Forest Hill by the otherwise inexplicable and nondescript 'Milton Stone', over the road from the Church of St Nicholas where the marriage took place. The village also has referential/reverential/residential cul-de-sacs called Milton Crescent and Powell Close.

John Wilmot

With the 1662 return of royal bottoms to vacant thrones, in the shape of supposedly Merry Monarch Charles II, an upwelling of new, bawdy, satirical entertainment took place, the puritanical cork having popped from the deep bottle of insults and toilet humour. John

Wilmot, 2nd Earl of Rochester (1647–80) was the foremost cracker of rude jokes, in the form of poetry and drama.

Oxfordshire through and through, Wilmot was born in Ditchley, educated at Oxford's Wadham College, had a large estate at Adderbury, and later lived at Spelsbury. Precocious, he gained his Masters degree at the age of fourteen, and was said to have entered into debauchery during those teenage years. This set him up well for a role in Charles II's so-called 'Merry Gang' of court jesters-cum-hellraisers. He managed to get banished from court a couple of times – once for writing a satire on the King, blaming his obsession with sex on the sad state of the country.

During his second exile in 1676, Wilmot assumed the alter-egos of Doctor and Mrs Bendo, for the sole purpose of examining female patients in penetrating detail. By 1680 it was all over. A combination of venereal diseases and alcoholism led to his death at Woodstock, aged thirty-three. He is buried at Sparsholt, and gained posthumous fame for his supposed deathbed renunciation of atheism and dissoluteness, ordering that his lewd works be gathered up and burnt. None of this prevented his spectacularly obscene play (although authorship is disputed) *Sodom, or the Quintessence of Debauchery* from surviving, one rare copy fetching £45,600 at Sotheby's in 2004.

Thomas Warton

Thomas Warton (1728–90), Poet Laureate, rector of Kiddington, fellow of Trinity College, and best known for his Oxford tribute *The Triumph of Isis*, had an interesting slant on the appropriate drinks to sip when reading:

> As there are here books suited to every taste, so there are liquors adapted to every species of reading. Amorous tales may be perused over *arrack punch* and *Jellies*; insipid elegies, over *orgeat* or *capilaire*; politics, over *coffee*; divinity, over *port*; and defence of bad generals and bad ministers, over *whipt syllabubs* … we may pronounce, in a literal sense, that learning remains no longer a dry pursuit.

Boom boom.

Warton was not averse to smuttier stuff either. In explaining where the best lessons in Oxford were to be found, he said: 'The doctrine of the screw is practically explained most evenings in the private rooms, together with the Motion of Fluids.'

Percy Bysshe Shelley

Legend says that Percy Bysshe Shelley (1792–1822) only ever attended one lecture at University College, but read for sixteen hours a day. One of his favourite spots during his brief stay at Oxford was Shotover Hill. He liked to gaze into a certain pool, an old quarry working, at dusk. According to an 1832 report, he could be observed there 'repeating verses aloud, or loudly exulting in the splash of the stones he continually threw'.

Matthew Arnold

When poet Matthew Arnold visited Boar's Hill near Oxford in the 1840s, with poet Arthur Hugh Clough, the elevated spot offered uninterrupted fine views of the city and its 'dreaming spires'.

Arnold, who became Oxford Professor of Poetry, hit upon the now timeless phrase in his poem 'Thyrsis: a Monody', in 1865. It was written in memory of Clough, and has sent several generations of romantics to the spot since publication – although Clough himself had written of the site as barren and depressing beneath grey February skies. Boar's Hill was also the setting of Arnold's equally celebrated poem 'The Scholar Gipsy', in which he wrote of the height from which 'the eye travels down to Oxford's towers'.

Chilswell near Cumnor used to be called Childsworth, and that is the name Matthew Arnold uses in 'Thyrsis'. The poem also mentions 'The signal-elm, that looks on Ilsley Downs'. The 'signal-elm' is still to be seen in a field near Chilswell (as is the best view of the dreaming spires). The site has been purchased by the Oxford Preservation Society, which has a cluster of sites here in the Boar's Hill vicinity. The tree is notable for the fact that it is not an elm at all, but an oak.

Boar's Hill

Numerous poets have since made Boar's Hill their home. Residents since the 1880s include Margaret Louisa Woods, Robert Bridges and John Masefield (successive Poet Laureates). Then came Masefield's tenant Robert Graves, and Edmund Blunden, both destined to become Oxford Professors of Poetry.

Other artists on the Hill include Gilbert Murray, the pre-eminent translator of Greek literature in the early twentieth century, in addition to countless other writings. Jewish Croatian sculptor Oscar Nemon (1906–85) lived here, most famous for his statues of Sir Winston Churchill. He also made a bust of Max Beerbohm, who taught him English after flight from the Nazis had brought him to the sanctuary of Oxford.

Sir Arthur Evans lived here too – the archaeologist who discovered and practically reinvented the ancient civilisation of the Minoans of Crete. In this same spirit of reinvention, Evans built Jarn Mound on Boar's Hill, in an attempt to produce a vantage point from which the 'dreaming spires' could look their best. Aspects of Evans' work can be seen in Oxford's Ashmolean Museum. Sadly, his Boar's Hill house, Youlbury, burnt down; as did, oddly enough, those of Margaret Woods, Robert Bridges and Gilbert Murray.

William Winwood Reade

The 'Druidical stone circle' at Ipsden House was erected in 1827, at a time when Druidism was being rediscovered (reinvented would be more accurate). The Reade family, who still own the house, created the monument; and William Winwood Reade (1838–75) wrote several books on the subject of Druidism. He is buried at St Mary's Church in Ipsden.

William led a very adventurous life, travelling in Africa and studying gorillas and human tribes. His most celebrated ordeal was a three-month stint as a prisoner of West African King Seedwa of Falaba. The King set Reade several sadistically difficult tasks to test his physical and mental strength, and legend has it that Reade triumphed.

The indomitable prisoner went on to produce twenty books, ranging from travel and anthropological accounts, to the aforementioned Druidism and novels. The most famous (and still in print) is his atheist history, *The Martyrdom of Man* (1872).

William Winwood Reade's greatest accolade comes from no lesser a thinker than Sherlock Holmes who, in *The Sign of Four* (1890), discussing the subject of statistical probability, declares: 'Winwoode Reade is good upon the subject.' Holmes also recommends *The Martyrdom of Man.*

William Morris

The artist William Morris, educated at Exeter College in Oxford, is remembered largely for his curtain and wallpaper patterns, like some nineteenth-century forerunner of Laura Ashley. But Morris's designs were revolutionary in their day, and that is a more accurate image of the man. He founded the Socialist League in 1884, and advocated a new society based on a shared love of nature; an absence of money, property and class; and all the other trappings of socialist utopia.

These ideas were expressed in his novel *News from Nowhere* (1890), whose setting was inspired by Kelmscott, Morris's spiritual home, where he was buried in 1896. He named his London residence Kelmscott House in honour of the village, and founded the Kelmscott Press there as a showcase of his artistry.

Edward Lear
According to Edward Lear (1812–88):

> There was an old soldier of Bicester,
> Was walking one day with his sister,
> A bull, with one poke,
> Toss'd her into an oak,
> Before the old gentleman miss'd her.

Flora Thompson
Juniper Hill near Cottisford, just south of the Northamptonshire border, was the birthplace of Flora Thompson (1876–1947). She renamed the hamlet 'Lark Rise' in her semi-autobiographical books, Cottisford itself becoming Fordlow. Her other key locations were Candleford (Buckingham) and Fringford (Candleford Green). Thompson's great loves were Jane Austen and the English countryside, which pretty much sums up her output. The books capture lives at once ordinary and meaningful, soaked in a rich four-season marinade of quintessential Englishness, a marriage of Vaughan Williams and Camberwick Green.

The *Lark Rise* trilogy (*Heatherley*, a sequel, appeared posthumously) started life as a series of essays published by Oxford University Press in 1938–43 as a healing balm to a nation suffering in wartime. Since then it has never been out of print, and it has inspired stage shows, music and the enormously popular *Lark Rise* TV series screened between 2008 and 2011 and filmed in Gloucestershire and Wiltshire. Online petitions were set up to persuade the BBC to continue the soapy drama, but so far to no avail.

William Butler Yeats
Irish poet and Nobel Laureate of Literature, William Butler Yeats, is commemorated in Thame with a Blue Plaque. Cuttlebrook House is where he lived during 1921, and where his son Michael Butler Yeats, Irish Senator, was born. Not the best of fathers, Yeats senior did all he

could to avoid being in the same place as his two children, deeming them 'little bundles of noise and infection'.

The plaque was unveiled in 2008, making amends in some way for the cul-de-sac named after the poet in the early 1990s, which was misspelled 'Yeates Close' on the extant street sign.

John Buchan

Scottish author John Buchan, 1st Baron Tweedsmuir (1875–1940), lived, and was buried, at Elsfield. A graduate of Brasenose College, best remembered for his novel *The Thirty-Nine Steps*, he spent the last five years of his life as Governor General of Canada, the monarch's official representative in that country. He was given a State funeral over there, but had requested that his ashes be flown home to beloved Elsfield. The manor there has a Blue Plaque commemorating his residence.

Buchan loved the countryside of Oxfordshire, and its capital city. Recalling his 1894 epiphany in the city, during a snowfall on Merton Street and Holywell, he later wrote: 'In that hour Oxford claimed me, and her bonds have never been loosed.'

The Thirty-Nine Steps was the first of five Buchan novels to feature stiff-upper-lipped detective action-hero Richard Hannay. The character has featured in a number of movies, and in the 1980s' TV series *Hannay*.

Agatha Christie

In 1934, Agatha Christie and her archaeologist husband Max Mallowan bought the early eighteenth-century Winterbrook House at Winterbrook near Wallingford. It became the model for Danemead, her detective Miss Marple's house in the fictional village of St Mary Mead. Christie died here in 1976, after writing close to 100 books and twenty-odd plays. She is buried in the church at nearby Cholsey. After her death, Mallowan married his long-term mistress Barbara Parker, both dying at Winterbrook too. Mallowan was buried beside Agatha.

C.S. Lewis

Oxford professor and Narnia creator Clive Staples Lewis was known as Jack to his friends and family. At the age of four he had lost his pet dog Jacksie in a road accident, and insisted on adopting the animal's name. The love of animals stayed with him, and he admitted that his earliest literary and creative influences were the anthropomorphic creations of Beatrix Potter.

Graduating at University College Oxford, Lewis taught at Magdalen College from 1925–54 before transferring to Cambridge. His biggest legacy in modern Oxford is the C.S. Lewis Nature Reserve at Risinghurst, formerly the grounds of his house The Kilns, a private residence which bears a Blue Plaque to the scholar-author.

J.R.R. Tolkien

John Ronald Reuel Tolkien was an Oxford University academic who had no interest in fame and celebrity, and yet who, in 2009, was judged the highest-earning dead celebrity in the world, on account of book sales and other Middle Earth merchandise and movie-related stuff.

Tolkien was a graduate of Exeter College; Rawlinson and Bosworth Professor of Anglo-Saxon based at Pembroke College, 1925–45; and Merton Professor of English Language and Literature from then until 1959, with earlier stints writing for the Oxford English Dictionary. Oxford currently has a J.R.R. Tolkien Professor of English Literature and Language post, in memory of the man's work and influence.

The ultimately melancholy tone of Tolkien's fictional works – his Legendarium, as he called it – derives from his circumstances: he began writing *The Book of Lost Tales*, his first inroads into the Middle Earth universe, whilst recovering from the Battle of the Somme in 1916. In terms of prose style, Tolkien later revealed that he was trying to echo the tone of William Morris and his *News from Nowhere*.

Tolkien is buried with his wife Edith in the cemetery at Wolvercote in north Oxford, and there are Blue Plaques on his one-time residences at 76 Sandfield Road and 20 Northmoor Road in suburban Oxford. His favourite city watering hole, the Eagle and Child on St Giles', is a busy beery shrine for pilgrims of Tolkien and his close friend C.S. Lewis.

Beyond Oxford, one of Tolkien's favourite pubs was the Bell inn at Charlbury. Drinking here in the 1950s, with his name in the literary firmament following the success of *The Lord of the Rings*, he overheard the landlord bemoaning his treatment by the brewery and wishing he could buy out the lease. Feeling magnanimous, Tolkien declared, 'I might be able to help you there, you know.' Not knowing who he was, the landlord assessed his customer's shabby appearance, wafted away the clouds of pipe smoke and replied curtly, 'Oh no, I don't think you can,' blowing what was probably his only chance of breaking free from the brewery yoke.

Nancy Mitford

Novelist and biographer Nancy Mitford (1904–73) was raised at Asthall Manor, and later at nearby Swinbrook Hall, which her father David Freeman-Mitchell, 2nd Baron Redesdale, built in 1926. The fictional Alconleigh in one of her most famous works, *The Pursuit of Love* (1945), is based on Asthall.

Nancy Mitford is rather unfairly celebrated and/or vilified as the editor-writer of the guide to correct upper-class behaviour, *Noblesse Oblige: An Enquiry into the Identifiable Characteristics of the English Aristocracy*. In it she points out 'U' and 'non-U' usages, in what was intended as a light-hearted celebration of the English language, a complement to her already established brand of 'Mitford' humour. But it was – and still is – taken as a bible of aristocratic verbal behaviour for the social climber, i.e. how to avoid sounding middle class. Examples of pitfalls to avoid include the non-U terms *toilet*, *dinner* and *lounge*, whose 'U' forms are *lavatory* or *loo*, *lunch* and *drawing-room*. One should say 'Good health' and not 'cheers', 'How d'you do?' and not 'Pleased to meet you', and 'jam' rather than the supposedly posh 'preserve'.

Nancy Mitford's other non-claim to fame was the script for the Ealing Studios film *Kind Hearts and Coronets* (1949). She was hired to write it, but none of her work made it into the finished production. Unbeknown to Mitford, Evelyn Waugh had been hired to do exactly the same thing ... but none of his work made it into the film either.

Nancy Mitford, along with two of her five sisters, is buried at the churchyard in Swinbrook.

Blewbury

Blewbury has been the home of diverse literary residents and their fictional beasts, including Kenneth Grahame's *Wind in the Willows* menagerie; Barbara Euphan Todd's Worzel Gummidge; and Dick Francis' best-selling racing horses.

George Orwell

Sutton Courtenay's All Saints' Church is the last resting place of author George Orwell (1903–50). As a boy he had frequented the area, sometimes fishing in the river; but the village was not the obvious choice of gravesite. Henley-on-Thames or Shiplake, where he spent some of his early years, might have been more appropriate.

Orwell's posthumous journey to Sutton was convoluted. Legend says that he wanted to be buried in the churchyard nearest to where he died. Passing away in London, it seemed that the choice of gravesites would be endless. The funeral service took place at Christ Church near Regent's Park, but the city could not find space for him and cremation seemed the only option – a fate that Orwell had expressly forbidden.

David Astor, Orwell's old friend from the *Observer* newspaper, stepped in. Based in palatial accommodation at Sutton Courtenay, Astor commanded the ear of the village vicar. Orwell was duly interred, with his real name, Eric Arthur Blair, inscribed on the headstone as he had instructed. Astor was later buried here too, alongside Orwell.

John Betjeman

By all accounts, Poet Laureate John Betjeman (1906–84) did not enjoy his studies at Magdalen College in Oxford. But his stint there left its mark on literature. Amongst his college baggage was a Teddy bear called Archibald Ormsby-Gore, who caught the eye of fellow student Evelyn Waugh. Waugh later cast Ormsby-Gore as Aloysius, the Teddy bear of Sebastian Flyte in *Brideshead Revisited*.

Betjeman himself captured the Oxford era in his long narrative poem 'Summoned by Bells', and his other works include many references to Oxfordshire locations. But he never quite recovered from his academic failures in the city, levelling ire at tutor C.S. Lewis. The only qualification he ever wrested from the University was an honorary doctorate, handed over in 1974.

Betjeman set his children's book *Archie and the Strict Baptists* in Uffington and Farnborough, the scenes of his childhood. The 'Archie' in question is that self-same bear Ormsby-Gore who, along with another favourite toy, Jumbo the elephant, was in Betjeman's arms when he died.

From 1972 to his death in 1984, Betjeman lived in Wantage. Wantage repaid its debt with the Betjeman Millennium Park, where his poem 'On Leaving Wantage' is carved in stone.

Binsey

Binsey is famous for three things – the picturesque pub the Trout, as visited by Colin Dexter's Inspector Morse; the trees mourned by Gerard Manley Hopkins in his poem 'Binsey Poplars'; and St Margaret's Church. The latter contains the ancient Treacle Well. This title used to denote nothing more than a curative well, 'treacle' being a word for a healing balm; but Lewis Carroll found the name irresistible, and used it as the basis for the sticky Treacle Well in *Alice's Adventures in Wonderland*.

Siobhan Dowd

The churchyard at St Margaret's is the last resting place of Siobhan Dowd, the children's author who died tragically young in 2007. Her second novel, *The London Eye Mystery*, posthumously won awards, as did her two subsequent published works, *Bog Child* scooping the Carnegie Medal in 2009. Her last manuscript, *A Monster Calls*, was completed by author Patrick Ness and released to great acclaim in 2011.

MUSICAL INTERLUDE

Joseph Haydn

In 1791, the prolific composer Joseph Haydn received an honorary doctorate from Oxford University. To mark the occasion, he conducted his Symphony no. 92, thereafter known as the Oxford Symphony (it being part of the agreement that receipt of the doctorate would involve him conducting three of his works). The Symphony wasn't actually written with Oxford in mind at all. Haydn had previously conducted the work in Paris and had not yet started work on his portfolio of 'English' pieces (the twelve 'London Symphonies'), and so for the Oxford event he simply led with his latest big hit. Many of the musicians in that performance were already familiar with the work, which, since there was no time for rehearsal, was very handy indeed.

Lucy Broadwood

Edwardian folk song collector Lucy Broadwood collected several gems in Oxfordshire – but the struggle to save these old songs from oblivion was an uphill one. Commenting on one of her sources, she noted:

> The singer, Mrs Vaisey, knew numbers of excellent old songs. When I expressed a hope that her children would learn them she said, 'They like to pick them up from me, and I like the old ballads myself, but my husband he says, "Don't teach them that rubbish! Give them *Hymns Ancient and Modern*!"'

Traffic

In the 1960s, über-hippies Steve Winwood, Jim Capaldi, Dave Mason and Chris Wood, aka the rock band Traffic, established their band-cum-commune at a cottage near Aston Tirrold. It was a secular chapter of a village whose history is steeped in religious unconformity (*see* p.52).

George Harrison

From the demise of The Beatles in 1970 until his death in 2001, George Harrison lived at the late nineteenth-century mansion Friar Park in Henley-on-Thames. Friends were often treated to Harrison's ukulele, on which he was able to play most of The Beatles' repertoire. This traced back to his early days in Liverpool, when fellow Lancastrian George Formby (d.1961) was uke-toting star of the airwaves. For Harrison, it was not just an affectation: he attended George Formby Society and Ukulele Society of Great Britain meetings, and since his patronage the instrument has undergone a renaissance.

North Stoke

North Stoke has celebrity connections – in addition to the not-very-musical actor Michael Caine, two contrasting vocalists were once resident here: opera singer Dame Clara Butt in the mid-twentieth century, and Ian Gillan of rock band Deep Purple. In true rock and roll fashion, Gillan had a guitar-shaped swimming pool built in the extensive grounds of his house, currently the Springs Hotel & Golf Club.

Holywell Music Rooms

Oxford's Holywell Music Rooms, opened in 1748, was the country's first purpose-built music venue. Today there are thousands of venues, and several hundred recording studios.

The Manor Studio

The manor at Shipton-on-Cherwell, which closed in 1995 and is currently the country residence of the Marquess of Headfort, has its place in rock music's hall of fame. In the 1970s it belonged to Richard Branson, who was looking for something to raise the profile of his embryonic record label Virgin. In 1972, along came Mike Oldfield, a reclusive figure with an off-the-wall concept album idea. The Manor Studio was put at his disposal – and Tubular Bells and sales figures of countless millions followed.

Fairport Convention

Although originally formed in Muswell Hill, London, and named after a house there, Fairport Convention has been associated with Oxfordshire for over forty years. Their singer, Sandy Denny (who died in 1978), lived at Cropredy in the early 1970s, and when their album *Nine* (1973) featured a photo of the band outside the Brasenose Arms in that village, the seal was set.

Various other members have lived in and around the village, and since 1980 it has hosted the annual music festival (currently called Fairport's Cropredy Convention) every second weekend in August. Ironically, it all began in 1979 when the band finished their 'Farewell' tour with a gig in Cropredy. Having seen their audiences diminish over the years, they had decided to quit while they were behind. But the last gig was so successful that they decided to do it all again the next year; and since then they've never looked back.

Festivals

In 1933, Kingsey in Oxfordshire was handed over to Buckinghamshire, and at the same time Towersey switched from Bucks to Oxfordshire. Towersey is best known these days for its musical connections. DJ Ken Bruce lives here, and the Village Festival has been running since 1965 – one of the biggest folk festivals in the country. Towersey Morris has been flourishing for more than fifty years too.

Oxfordshire is certainly not short of other music festivals. To merely scratch the surface:

Oxford Jazz Festival: four-day April extravaganza in great locations
Oxford Music Festival: April/May, classical showcase with lectures
Dorchester-on-Thames Festival: May, and 'Midsomer Murders' trails too
English Music Festival: more classical brilliance at Dorchester
Faringdon Arts Festival: July, inspired by eccentric Lord Berners (*see* p.23)
Henley Festival: July, classical to family-friendly rock, week after the regatta
Cornbury Music Festival: Great Tew, July, rural eclectic rock and related
Arcane Festival: September, Eynsham, rustic, small, affordable
Oxford Summer Fayre Festival: September, Radio One-friendly in South Park
Truck Festival: Steventon, September, rock and indie for young at heart
Oxford Chamber Music Festival: September, what it says on the label

BRUSH WITH FAME

William Turner

William Turner (1789–1862) is often dubbed 'Turner of Oxford' to differentiate him from the more famous, and not entirely dissimilar, J.M.W. Turner. He was born at Black Bourton, lived for many years at the manor house in Shipton-on-Cherwell, and ended his days on St John's Street in Oxford (commemorated by a Blue Plaque). He was buried in Holy Cross churchyard at Shipton, having designed the new building during the Victorian Gothic revival onslaught. The 'of Oxford' tag is highly apt, as his most celebrated works involve, or are informed by, views and details of the landscape around the city.

Jane Burdon

Oxford's Jane Burdon was born on 19 October 1839 in St Helen's Passage (leading from New College Lane to the Turf Tavern). Its alternative name was Hell Passage, a comment on its slums. But Burdon's was a Cinderella tale, and at the age of eighteen her striking features won her the hearts of Pre-Raphaelite Brotherhood painters Rossetti and Burne-Jones. She was roped in to pose as Guinevere in their Oxford Union Arthurian murals.

Another member of the Brotherhood was William Morris. Rossetti fell in love with Burdon, but it was Morris who married her, at St Michael's Church, Cornmarket, in 1859. After this, glass slipper firmly in place, Burdon was educated and socially equipped for her new status; and she became the one and only face for the Pre-Raphaelite artists, and is still instantly recognisable.

Things began to unwind in 1871 when Morris and Rossetti rented Kelmscott Manor in Oxfordshire, Rossetti and Burdon continuing their love affair. She survived the turmoil; and, rich and famous, eventually bought the manor in 1913 for her daughter. She is buried in the village churchyard; and there is a Blue Plaque to her in St Helen's Passage.

L.S. Lowry

L.S. Lowry (1887–1976) frequently visited the county to stay with his Carterton sister. He was never inspired to paint the place though; although he did manage a quick Witney.

Conroy Maddox

Conroy Maddox spent some of his childhood in Chipping Norton, painting his early pictures in a room at his parents' flat over the

Blue Boar pub. These were controversial works, however, Maddox having embraced the surrealist movement of Salvador Dali and his followers. So weird did his creations appear to contemporary eyes that suspicions were aroused. During the Second World War, having gazed in dull-eyed confusion at his works, Scotland Yard declared that Conroy Maddox was a Fifth Columnist, seeking to sabotage the Allied war effort through coded messages in his paintings. It was, indeed, the most surreal incident in his artistic life. He died in 2005, aged ninety-two.

Wittenham Clumps

The twin peaks of Wittenham Clumps near Dorchester-on-Thames are hilly bits in the flatlands of the Thames Valley. They form part of a complex of ancient landmarks taking in Neolithic, Bronze and Iron Age forts and tumuli, and even a mosaic-floored Romano-British house (uncovered by TV's *Time Team* in 2004). The two eminences – Round Hill and Castle Hill – belong to a larger range called the Sinodun Hills, from the British words *seno dunum*, meaning 'old fort'. The site has also been known as the Clumps, the Berkshire Bubs (i.e. boobs), and Mother Dunch's Buttocks, a reference to a bottom-heavy Lady of the Manor in the seventeenth century.

Wittenham Clumps have inspired many artists over the years. In the summers of 1844 and 1845, Joseph Tubb, a wood carver-cum-maltster from Warborough, camped out on Castle Hill and carved a twenty-line poem into the bark of an extant beech – the Poem Tree. The wooden stanzas can still be read. Tubb was passionate about the local countryside, and had done a stint in Oxford Prison after pulling down fences erected to enclose common ground.

Matthew Prior wrote on the Clumps too, although he used the more conventional pencil and paper; another literary feat marked with a plaque. Artist Paul Nash (1889–1946) painted the spot several times in the twentieth century.

5

CRIME AND PUNISHMENT

PRISONS AND COURTS

Courts of Assize

Serious criminal cases used to be judged at the Courts of Assize. In 1972 these were replaced by the Crown Court, as were the regional Quarter Sessions. Held four times a year, the latter filtered out the serious cases, which were then passed to the Assizes. Oxford was the county's Assize town, providing lengthy, gory material for the local press. The Quarter Sessions were held in Oxford and Banbury.

Magistrates' Courts

Minor offences were processed by Justices of the Peace at Magistrates' Courts, or 'Petty Sessions'. In addition, the towns had various cells and dungeons, and larger villages had lock-ups for drunkards and other anti-socials. The windowless pyramidal folly near the children's playground in Wheatley is a fine survival of the village lock-up.

Bawdy Courts

The moral police had their own means of punishing offenders – at 'Bawdy Courts', such as the one at Banbury. They were an early version of the extant ecclesiastical court which settles Church matters relating to property and disciplinaries. Prior to the mid-nineteenth century, these courts also censured such activities as adultery, heresy, witchcraft, prostitution, drunkenness, fornication and working on Sundays.

Oxford Castle

Oxford Castle was owned by Christ Church College until 1785, when the city magistrates purchased the site. It had been used as a prison since the civil wars of the previous century, and, like most gaols of the day, it was mainly a place to hold prisoners pending trial. Their fate after this was usually execution or transportation; but, after the American War of Independence, and with the American predilection for African slaves, the usual port for transportees, Virginia, was

Ancient northern entrance into Oxford, with the Bocardo Prison over the gate.

suddenly closed. Until Australia and New Zealand became viable options, English prisons could barely soak up the excess bodies.

Oxford's prison was certainly in a sorry state in 1785, when magistrates set about repairing and restructuring the site. They appointed Daniel Harris (1760–1840) as Clerk of Works, but he immediately fell out with the prison governor, Solomon Wisdom. The main dispute seems to have been over the positioning of the prison dunghill. There was little wisdom in Solomon's opposition: he was sacked, and Harris took his place.

Daniel Harris continued the building works, dabbled in archaeological investigation at the site, produced illustrations for the University's annual Oxford Almanac, and married into a wealthy local family. Local boy dung good, you might say.

Oxford Prison released its last inmates in 1996, and in 2006 the prison and castle complex was reopened as a tourist attraction and restaurant.

HMP Huntercombe

A prison camp was built at Huntercombe, near Henley, in the Second World War – its star inmate being, albeit briefly, Rudolf Hess in 1941. Hess had flown to Scotland in a Messerschmitt (and crash-landed) in an attempt to negotiate with the British. Huntercombe was one of the places he was held before being delivered to the Tower of London. The fact that Hitler said he was to be shot if he ever returned to Germany won Hess – once the Führer's heir apparent – a kind of grudging respect in Britain.

In 1946 the Oxfordshire site opened as HMP Huntercombe, although the wartime buildings have now disappeared. The county's other prison is Bullingdon at Arncott near Bicester. It opened in 1992, and overcrowding has been a constant problem.

Old Gaol in Abingdon

The Old Gaol in Abingdon was built by Napoleonic prisoners of war. Completed in 1811, it was Berkshire's sole prison for the next fifty years and claims to be the building that set the pattern of British prisons, based on a central core with cell-block wings extending outwards. It closed in 1868, and by 1874 was being used as a grain store. It is now a flats-and-shops development.

EARLY OFFENDERS

Beckley church

Beckley church has the county's oldest depictions of crime and punishment. In 1845, some fourteenth-century fire-and-brimstone murals were uncovered on the walls, but Victorian sensibilities allowed the lurid images to succumb once again to dust and dirt. In 1933 they were revealed once more in their gory glory. The highlight of the mural is a naked body being roasted and basted by two demons. A third pumps the bellows to keep the flames alive. Whether this brought to mind everlasting perdition or the pressing practicalities of Sunday lunch, we shall never know.

Combe and South Leigh churches

Similar unpleasantries are to be found in a fifteenth-century painting at Combe church – a 'Doom', depicting a poker-faced Christ and a crowd of souls on the Day of Judgement. South Leigh near Witney also has a 'Doom' in its fifteenth-century portfolio. Here too the dead are judged, using the ancient motif of weighing the soul. It was first painted in the fourteenth century: its predecessor is just visible behind the much bigger replacement.

Piers Gaveston

Poker-faced Judgement is often usurped by mob rule. On 9 June 1312, a weary party stopped at an inn in Deddington, several days into their trek south from Scarborough Castle. In their midst was Piers Gaveston, favourite of King Edward II, a hate figure for a large group of rebellious earls. Gaveston's personal gaoler, the Earl of Pembroke, had promised to let him live, as long as he forfeited the vast lands Edward had given him.

But when Pembroke took the opportunity to visit his wife at nearby Brampton, Gaveston's enemies surrounded the inn. His apathetic guards refused to defend him and he was forced to surrender to the Earl of Warwick, his bitterest enemy. Ten days after his stay in Deddington, after being chained and imprisoned, Gaveston was stabbed to death and beheaded at Blacklow Hill in Warwickshire. Deddington's coat of arms shows a black eagle in chains, a reference to poor Piers and the judgement of his peers.

Gallowstree Common

Chains and gibbets livened up many lonely Oxfordshire roads. Gallowstree Common in the Kidmore parish was aptly named. The tree in question was a large oak opposite a barn, and the gibbet and chains were still hanging there in the late eighteenth century. The last man to swing in the chains had been convicted for sheep stealing, a capital offence prior to Queen Victoria's reign.

Anne Green

Before the innovation of the 'Drop', by which a hanged prisoner was launched to a swift death from a height, hanging was painfully drawn out. Hoisted by the rope, the victim would often suffer before death. Anne Green was one such victim in 1650, after being found guilty of killing her newborn baby. She had been seduced and abandoned by the son of her employer, and the baby was probably stillborn. These extenuating circumstances were noted at the trial, but Anne was hanged nonetheless in Oxford's Cattle Yard on 14 December.

While she was choking, the spectators swung from her legs so energetically that the crowd had to be dispersed, out of fear that the gallows would break. After half an hour or so, Anne Green was declared dead and the body was cut down.

It came as a great surprise when Anne revived. She had been placed in a coffin and carted off for dissection at the University's Anatomy School. Three doctors had gathered by the coffin, scalpels poised – but when the lid was lifted Anne took a rasping breath, and the doctors attempted resuscitation, employing hot drinks, blood-letting, massage, compression of the arms and legs, and hot bandages. She was then placed in a bed with another woman, whose purpose was to keep the patient warm.

After twelve hours, Anne spoke; and over the next few days she regained her memory, her swollen face returned to normal and her motor functions were slowly restored. News of the recovery spread, and, accepting it all as a weird miracle, the Oxford justices reprieved the poor woman.

Anne Green later married and had three children, keeping her coffin as a macabre souvenir. She survived her own execution by fifteen years.

Protestant martyrs

The county's most famous executions took place in the reign of Queen Mary I. In October 1555, in a violent attempt to remedy the Protestant lurch of her brother Edward VI's reign, the Catholic Queen's court condemned three men – Bishops Hugh Latimer and Nicholas Ridley and Archbishop Thomas Cranmer – to burn at the stake in Oxford. The alleged spot on Broad Street (in the former town ditch) is marked with a cross on the road.

Latimer and Ridley went to the flames first, Ridley telling his friend that God would either reduce the heat of the flames or bolster their spirits to withstand the pain. Latimer, reassured, told his companion at the bonfire: 'Be of good cheer, Ridley, and play the man. We shall this day, by God's grace, light up such a candle in England, as I trust, will never be put out.'

But it was Cranmer's death in March 1556 that produced the most striking image for local legend. This former Archbishop of Canterbury had at one point recanted on paper, out of fear for his life; but facing the flames, he now declared: 'This is the hand that wrote it, and therefore shall it suffer first punishment.' As the fire mounted, Cranmer allowed his right hand to burn. Sources say he cried out, 'This hand hath offended!' throughout.

SOME NOTABLE CRIMINALS
AND THEIR CRIMES

Bartholomew Steer

In 1592, as part of her itinerary through Oxfordshire, Elizabeth I visited Sir Henry Lee (former Queen's Champion and MC at her accession festivities) at his house in Ditchley. Lee staged an old-fashioned two-day spectacle of tilting, chivalric pursuits and other fripperies.

Fast forward to 1596 ... Ditchley is now a deserted village, enclosures having robbed the villagers of their resources, compounded by 1596's poor harvests and corresponding high prices. Bartholomew Steer, carpenter from Hampton Poyle, leads the anti-enclosure Oxfordshire Rising, planning a visit to the former Queen's Champion Henry Lee, along with other rich property owners of the region, with the intention of beheading them and then marching to London as part of a larger rebellion.

The Rising was soon brought down. John Barry, Lord of the Manor of Hampton Gay, was tipped off by a local carpenter who possibly wished to see the competition axed, literally. The Oxfordshire Rising's ringleaders were arrested, and Steer was sentenced to be hanged, drawn and quartered.

The Rising wasn't without positive repercussions, however: it led directly to the Tillage Act of 1597, which restored much arable land lost to pasture. Parliament stated that 'order should be taken about inclosures ... that the poor may be able to live'.

This didn't stem the tide for long, though, and the enclosures continued through to the nineteenth century, much to the hardship and dismay of the commoners.

Mary Blandy

Kingston Bagpuize House, these days a popular venue for weddings and other functions, was the residence of John Blandy in the eighteenth century. His cousin Mary was a frequent visitor until, in 1752 at the age of thirty-one, she ceased to call, on account of being hanged on the gallows outside Oxford Prison. Her case caused a national media sensation at the time, and was still being re-examined 100 years later.

Mary had fallen in love with William Henry Cranston, an army officer and son of a Scottish nobleman – good credentials, you would think. But Mary's father did not approve of the match, causing his daughter to seek desperate remedies. She poisoned him with arsenic, claiming in court that she had intended the draft as a love potion to make her father approve of the marriage. This excuse did not save her, and, after being hounded pre-trial by crowds convinced of her guilt, Mary Blandy kept the newspapers and bloodthirsty public happy by becoming the last female hanged in public in Oxford.

In an oddly folkloric coda to the story, it is said that a blackbird perched on a beam of the scaffold during the hanging, since which time no blackbird has sung in the grounds of the old prison.

James Till

On 26 April 1754, James Till stood before the gallows at Oxford Castle. He had been found guilty of stealing 70 guineas from his employer. Till was only seventeen, and his death sentence had been reprieved twice, but a Royal Pardon was not forthcoming.

The crowd was angry at the injustice, and determined to save Till's body from the clutches of the University's Anatomy School. In March that year, a similar crowd – described as 'rioters' in the local newspaper – had rescued two dead bodies from the gallows, both of which had been earmarked by the Professor of Physick to provide graphic illustration during lectures. They had not been punished for abducting the corpses, however, largely due to the parliamentary elections that were taking place in the county. (Oxfordshire's Tory seats had been uncontested since 1710, and the audacity of Whigs putting forward candidates in 1752 had led to two years of new and highly distracting levels of pre-election bribery and corruption – a situation which inspired William Hogarth's satirical series of paintings, 'An Election', hanging at Sir John Soane's Museum in London.)

Buoyed on by the general feeling of disgust at the establishment, the 'rioters' were now back to transport James Till to a gentler posthumous resting place. The University, however, sent in the troops. The outcome of this battle of the body-snatchers was never in doubt, and Till's luckless corpse became the subject of an anatomical lecture.

John Billingsgate

This same Oxfordshire election of 1752–4 had resulted in hysterical propaganda from each side of the political divide. In July 1754, the fledgling *Jackson's Oxford Journal* joined the pro-Tory assault, printing an article detailing the punishment of a certain John Billingsgate. He was taken to a scaffold outside the newly opened

Town Hall in front of a baying mob of 'fish wives'. Throughout the proceedings he cursed and swore, as he had done throughout his life – a dissolute span spent indulging in gambling, cock pits, women of ill repute, extortion and murder.

Billingsgate made a contrite speech condemning his activities, after which his tongue was cut out. Jackson's rag reported:

> Upon taking out the tongue it blistered the hand that held it, and at several yards distance toasted cheese like a salamander: great quantities of water were then thrown upon it, but it was so much inflamed that it was impossible to quench it. Some dogs that came within its influence were seized with a sudden fit of barking and snarling; but what was odd was at the same time they lost the power of biting.

'Without a tongue I have no more chance in life than a cat in hell without claws,' Billingsgate wrote. In a sequel to the original article, he stated that he was 'Chaplain in Ordinary' at cock-fights at the Cock and Bottle, adding that he once fought an opponent publicly in his cassock.

John Billingsgate is fictional of course, and the satire appears to have been an attack on John Bilstone, a University clergyman and Whig. It is also linked to Oxford's Town Hall, which opened in 1754 on St Aldates, formerly known as Fish Street, Oxford's own version of Billingsgate in London. 'Billingsgate' confesses in the article that he has spent many hours employing 'unlawful nets' on the river in Port Meadow, 'not so much for the fish, but to spite the City by destroying the Breed, in revenge for being turned out of my Lectureship.'

Whatever the symbolism of all this, the two contested Oxfordshire seats, after much bribery and vote rigging, produced no clear winners. In 1755, the Whig majority in the Commons gave the seats to their candidates: another glorious chapter for democracy.

Isaac Darkin, aka Dumas

Reigning briefly as the county's most infamous highwayman, Dumas was arrested after a robbery near Nettlebed. Throughout his trial, and on the gallows, he showed great disdain and bravado, much to the delight of the crowd and the dismay of his female admirers, whose numbers had reached fan-club proportions. He was executed on 23 March 1761 – placing the rope round his own neck and leaping to his death before the executioner could intervene. His intention had been to emulate his hero – the fictional, unrepentantly villainous, Macheath from John Gay's hugely popular *Beggar's Opera* (1728). After being hanged and cut down, he was carried to St Thomas' Church in Oxford by a gang of bargemen. They filled the corpse with lime to prevent anatomisers getting their hands on Dumas – their scalpels had been his one fear.

Giles Covington

Twenty-one-year-old Giles Covington, seaman and petty criminal, was arrested for the murder of a pedlar at Abingdon. Richard Kilby, an army deserter suspected of the crime, pointed the finger at Giles and an accomplice, Charles Shury, in order to gain a Royal Pardon. Covington protested his innocence throughout the trial, writing contrite pleading letters from Oxford Prison. But the verdict was not overturned, and he hanged at Oxford on 7 March 1791. Prior to his death, he wrote a note stating: 'There only remains now for me to do justice to myself, by solemnly and truly declaring, in the presence of Almighty God, my entire innocence of the transaction for which I now suffer.'

Covington's corpse was afterwards used by medical students, and, in spite of numerous campaigns to get his name cleared and his remains buried, his wired bones are still hanging in the Museum of Oxford on Blue Boar Street.

George King

Circus guru 'Lord' George Sanger, in his 1910 autobiography *Seventy Years a Showman*, records that, on 17 October 1833, his father was drinking in the Red Lion in Wantage, having brought his travelling show to the Statute Fair. The town was renowned for violence and was nicknamed 'Black Wantage' – and that night in the Red Lion it affirmed its reputation.

Farm labourer George King entered the pub with a sickle and proceeded to argue with landlady Ann Pullen. When eventually she brought a conciliatory drink to his table, he threw some coins on the floor. The landlady bent down to pick them up, and King lopped off her head with a single stroke of his sickle.

It was a coup for Sanger. The following day, his show at the fair had mock-ups of the incident, dramatised as a peep-show for the grisly public as 'Murder at the Roadside Inn'.

But, like all dramatists, George Sanger meddled with the truth, either through faulty memory or for dramatic effect. The murder did indeed take place, but in the kitchen of the White Hart on Newbury Street on 30 August, the motive being simple robbery. At his arrest, a crooked sixpence was found in King's pockets, a distinctive coin known to have belonged to Ann Pullen. King confessed all and was hanged on 3 March 1834 at Oxford.

If Sanger's father staged the peep-show it must have been well after the event, and it is doubtful that he was present at the scene of the crime.

Dr W.C. Minor

James Augustus Henry Murray (1837–1915) began work on the first Oxford English Dictionary (OED) in 1878. Amongst his army of enthusiastic amateur researchers was the ultra efficient Dr W.C. Minor, who eventually contributed 12,000 quotations for the project. Organising a celebratory Dictionary Dinner at Oxford in October 1897, Murray was keen to invite and meet the elusive doctor.

Disappointingly, Minor replied that he was too ill to attend, but invited Murray to come to a mansion in Crowthorne, Berkshire. Murray took up the invitation, and was ushered into an impressively book-stuffed study. Approaching the sole figure in this private library, Murray declared what a pleasure it was to finally meet his indispensable contributor.

The owner of the mansion shook his hand, but announced that his name was Nicholson, and that he was the governor of Broadmoor Asylum for the Clinically Insane, just down the road in Crowthorne. Dr Minor, an American and former army surgeon, was his longest-serving inmate, committed here after being found guilty of murder.

It's a good story. Murray did eventually meet Minor – several times in fact – but the meeting at the governor's house is a piece of well-structured fiction.

None of which alters the fact that the mad doctor contributed enormously to the OED. Murray once declared of the madman's Minor contributions 'that we could easily illustrate the last four centuries from his quotations alone'.

John Stanley Phillips

The strangled and mutilated body of Harold Matthews, sixteen-year-old kitchen dogsbody, was discovered on the roof of Oxford University's Wycliffe Hall on 6 February 1938. Investigations quickly rooted out John Stanley Phillips, a religious zealot studying for Holy Orders, with a sideline in practical dissection. Questioned by officers, he declared: 'I had better confess. I am guilty.'

Phillips told his prison doctors that the planning of the murder had taxed him, and that he did not realise that cutting off Matthews' limbs would kill him. Quite what he intended doing with a limbless, living victim is something he did not divulge. Found guilty but insane, Phillips was imprisoned for life.

ALTERNATIVE PUNISHMENTS

Whip 'em

On the one hand, the comments of Sir William Anson of All Souls College, Oxford, the Chairman of the Oxfordshire Quarter Sessions in the 1890s, seem surprisingly benevolent and enlightened: 'I should say that of the modes of dealing with juvenile offenders … imprisonment should, if possible, be avoided,' he declared in response to an official report on juvenile offenders. But his concern was not child welfare; he was simply worried about the expense of locking them up.

Anson stressed that issuing fines merely led to imprisonment due to non-payment, and punished the parental wallet rather than the child. The children, he said, might indeed be punished – i.e. beaten – by their parents if they committed crimes and were made to pay fines; but, to ensure that none of them escaped, he advocated State-controlled whipping. It was the ASBO of its day. Anson concluded:

> Corporal Punishment is the cheapest form of punishment for the public, the least injurious to the character of the young offenders, and the most effectual deterrent. There should be no difficulty in regulating the administration of it, so as to avoid all risk of cruelty, or demoralising influences.

Name and shame 'em

'Young offenders' was a criminal tag coined by the Victorians. It was applied in September 1887 to ten-year-old Frederick Launchbury, charged with stealing 10s 6d from an Oxford shop to spend at St Giles' Fair. He was arrested there 'playing at cocoanuts', and the magistrates, deeming him a tough nut to crack, 'ordered the lad to be sent to the industrial training ship *Formidable*, lying off Bristol, to be trained for a sailor'.

The habit of type-casting people into various criminal groups – i.e. justifying contempt and distancing oneself from any responsibility towards the plight of the down-and-out – was nothing new. Amongst these groups, beggars have been stuffed into more pigeonholes than... well, pigeons. A cynical field guide-type pamphlet published in the mid-nineteenth century mentions a few:

> Shallow Coves ... are impostors begging through the country as shipwrecked sailors ... A few years since, a school of six shallow coves, who were at Oxford, obtained in one day in that city, thirteen suits of good clothes, besides a considerable sum of money. The clothes were all sold the same evening to dealers in old clothes. Oxford was at that time reckoned to be one of the best places in the kingdom for shallow coves.

> Shallow Mots are females who, like shallow coves, go nearly naked ... Some state that they have been robbed by a companion, or a fellow lodger, and great numbers of them represent themselves as being widows ... I have seen vast numbers of this class, and all, without exception, were not only addicted to drinking, but to everything else which is bad.

> Cadgers are those who make begging their trade ... There are among cadgers many men who have very good pensions ... A cadger who received his at Oxford, when I was there, got stupidly drunk, and was robbed the same night by some females ... and had to beg the next day for something to eat.

Transport 'em

In the early nineteenth century, the British colonies in Australia were in need of old-fashioned slave labour, much to the relief of the overcrowded prisons. At the Oxford Assizes, the justices did their best to feed demand by sending as many men overseas as possible. As a snapshot of this trend, the following sentences were listed in *Jackson's Oxford Journal*, 8 March 1828:

> William Bolton, 25, charged with receiving [stolen] property – fourteen years' transportation. James Lamb, 25, for stealing £12 19s 6d from the person of Rich. Henderson, at Cropredy – fourteen years' transportation. Edward Morris, 40, for stealing a pair of breeches, the property of John Allsop, of Wheatley – fourteen years' transportation. Richard Huck, 21, charged with breaking into a dwelling house ... at Fulbrook ... and stealing six £1 notes and a crown piece, seven years' transportation. James Hemmings,

21, charged with feloniously stealing from ... John Salmon, of Hardwick, a quantity of wearing apparel, his property – seven years' transportation. William Cranfield, 38, charged with stealing ... at Shiplake, a silver watch and two gold seals, value £5 – seven years' transportation. Eliza Stow, 15, charged with breaking open the dwelling house of James Savery, of Chadlington, and stealing a coral necklace, a net cap, a thimble case, &c. – seven years' transportation.

Relatively petty thefts such as these were the deeds that fed the colonies' transport needs. Bigger hauls, such as Charles Langford's £50 theft, reported at the same Assize, still brought the death penalty, as did the county's favourite occupation, sheep stealing.

Gamekeepers managed to collar many a potential transportee, and the deer parks of Shotover and Wychwood provided many. The Oxfordshire Sessions heard endless pleas, including a 1788 case where commoner Thomas James was gaoled for 'cruelly beating' three Wychwood gamekeepers. In 1824, assistant gamekeeper James Millin was murdered, and suspects were swiftly, possibly arbitrarily, rounded up. In 1836, Edmund Harding and William Stafford were transported to Australia for seven years, after being found guilty of assaulting a keeper.

Most of the trouble came from the forest dwellers themselves. In 1782, head keeper Gray had two deerhounds stolen from his forest lodge in Wychwood. Two days later, he found them hanging from a tree by their necks. It was assumed that this was a comment from his neighbours, rather than hungry outsiders.

Can't catch 'em ...

In September 1827, William Williams was on his way from Windsor to St Giles' Fair in Oxford to sell his wares. He was accosted near Wallingford by two men, with paper tucked under their hats and over their faces to hide their identities. They asked Williams what he was carrying, and, when he revealed it was a selection of spiced nuts to sell in Oxford, they asked if they could sample some.

After eating, they returned to their intended mugging, saying, 'If you have goods to sell, you have money to give away: we want money, and money we must have before we leave you, if not, we will knock you down with this stick.' Brandishing the relevant bludgeon over Williams' head, they continued: 'Let us have your money and your bundle, and we won't ill-use you; we know you very well, and when we are better off, we will return it to you again.'

Williams was robbed of 13s 6d, his nuts and his clothes. The muggers warned him to neither watch their retreat nor report their actions, or they would waylay him with violence. Needless to say, Williams never received the promised compensation.

The Ascott Martyrs

On the village green of Ascott-under-Wychwood, an octagonal bench built around a chestnut tree in 1973 commemorates the centenary of the Ascott Martyrs. The martyrs in question were all women, attempting in 1873 to support the National Union of Agricultural Workers (NUAW). Their husbands, complaining of poor working conditions and low pay, had gone on strike, resulting in mass sackings.

When the guilty farmer employed men from Ramsden to take their place, a sixteen-strong delegation of wives formed a picket line. Their efforts were rewarded with arrest, a swift trial at Chipping Norton, and imprisonment for a week in Oxford Castle with hard labour. Their children were looked after by neighbours, with NUAW assistance, during their incarceration.

The good folk of Chipping Norton rose up in protest, 1,000 of them gathering outside the police court – rioting, in the official reports of the day – in an unsuccessful attempt to get the women released. Three thousand gathered in Chipping Norton on the following day, where they were addressed by Joseph Arch, the most influential social reform speaker of the day. A whip-round coughed up £80 to support the women and their families.

Their efforts were eventually successful: questions in Parliament were followed by a Royal Pardon from Queen Victoria, who sent each woman 5s and a red flannel petticoat. The NUAW bettered this with £5 each and material to make a blue silk dress. The episode was used as a springboard to an investigation into labouring conditions on Oxfordshire farms.

Four of the martyrs upped sticks for New Zealand, where their proud descendants still live.

6

LEGENDS, SUPERSTITION AND THE SUPERNATURAL

STRANGE BUT NOT TRUE

White Horse

The 110m-long White Horse at Uffington, the famously disjointed chalk hillside figure, was long thought to have been scratched into the rock at the command of King Alfred the Great, while folklore said it represented the dragon defeated by St George on neighbouring Dragon Hill. Sober archaeologists, however, have dated it back 3,000 years to the Bronze Age.

Until the late nineteenth century, the White Horse was cleaned and scoured every seven years, and the event was the premise for a hilltop fair, as immortalised in Thomas 'Tom Brown's School Days' Hughes' book *The Scouring of the White Horse*. The beast has featured in many other writings, artworks and logos.

Although it looks very little like a horse, the chalk figure has been declared equine since at least the twelfth century. It is said to rise and graze in the grassland below the hill known as The Manger, which no self-respecting dragon would do.

Letcombe

In the ninth century, the Saxons defeated the Danes near the ancient Ridgeway path. Such was the slaughter that the blood ran down the hill like a stream, causing excited villagers below to shout 'Let it come!' This led to their settlement being named 'Let come', as in modern Letcombe Regis. However, even though the phrase 'let come' would have been comprehensible to the Anglo-Saxon ears of the villagers, 'Letcombe' probably means 'the stream in the valley'.

East and West Hagbourne

It is said that East and West Hagbourne used to be one village. But, in 1659, a fire destroyed all the houses in the centre of the settlement, and the surviving bits were never reunited. However, a cursory glance at historical records, including the 1086 Domesday Book, shows that East and West Hagbourne were always separate. The story originates in the fire that razed all of the thatched cottages in East Hagbourne, sparing only the church, on 10 March 1659.

Ride a cock horse to Banbury Cross
The nursery rhyme:

> Ride a cock horse to Banbury Cross
> To see a fine lady upon a white horse;
> With rings on her fingers and bells on her toes,
> She shall have music wherever she goes

is said to refer to seventeenth-century aristocrat Celia Fiennes (pronounced 'fines') – i.e. 'to see a Fiennes lady upon a white horse'. Celia was the sister of the 3rd Viscount Saye and Sele of nearby Broughton Castle. It has also been claimed that the rhyme refers to Queen Elizabeth I, who visited the town and was greeted by minstrels and merrymaking. She rode to the cross on horseback, her carriage having broken a wheel. This is all speculation, though, and the original printed version of 1784 has 'an *old* woman upon a white horse', rather than a fine one.

Otmoor
In the 1830s, Lord Abingdon's enclosure of Otmoor led to rioting. He had no legal right to the land, but the commoners didn't have strong legal legs to stand on either. Their 'time immemorial' claim to common rights on the moor hinged on a vague and unsubstantiated folk tale: the land was supposedly the gift of an ancient benefactress – a common figure in land tenure folklore – who donated to the public as much land as she could gallop round on horseback while an oat sheaf was burning. This led to the land being called Oatmoor, later Chinese-whispered to Otmoor.

Mr Fox
According to a local version of a very widespread folk tale generally called 'Mr Fox', a girl from Brewer's Lane in Oxford was in love with a student called Fox and was keen to marry him. The student was less enthusiastic and decided to kill her instead. He asked her to meet him by a certain tree on Divinity Walk in the city one moonlit night. The girl was suspicious, and, arriving purposefully early, she hid in the branches and waited for her lover to appear.

Fox, also arriving earlier than the planned tryst, brought a spade and dug a grave. He waited for his lover until dawn, but she remained hidden in the tree. The following day, Fox saw her in her doorway on Brewer's Lane. He asked why she had jilted him, and she replied:

> One moonshiney night as I sat high,
> Waiting for one to come by,
> The boughs did bend, my heart did ache
> To see what hole the fox did make.

Fox rushed at the poor poetess and killed her with a knife. Some townsmen tried to apprehend him, but other students took his side and a huge brawl ensued – one of the city's many 'Town versus Gown' riots. In the aftermath, the girl was buried exactly where the student had intended, in the grave beneath the tree on Divinity Walk.

FAIR ROSAMUND

When Henry II's lover 'Fair Rosamund' Clifford died in 1176, some said she had been poisoned by the jealous Queen Eleanor. The lovers' favourite meeting place was the specially constructed hunting lodge at Woodstock Palace. In legend it was at the centre of a labyrinth, which Eleanor navigated by following a trail of thread before delivering the deathly blow.

Henry had Rosamund buried at Godstow Nunnery, beside the altar. The tomb assumed shrine-like proportions that struck many as idolatry, and it was moved outside two years after Henry's death, where it managed to survive the sixteenth-century monastic suppression. It had upon it a punning rhyming couplet: *Hic jacet*

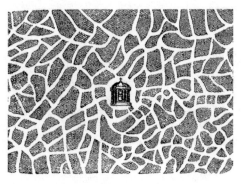

The stone labyrinth.

in tumba Rosamundi non Rosamunda, Non redolet sed olet, quae redolere solet, which translates as something like: 'Here lies in the tomb the rose of the world, not a pure rose: she who used to smell sweet still smells, but not sweetly.'

However, when the broken tomb was examined in 1631 it bore the simple inscription 'TUMBA ROSAMUNDAE'. Rosamund's bones were found to be wrapped in leather and encased in lead. A pleasing fragrance rose from them, in spite of the cruel rhyme.

Having physically (if not spiritually) survived the Reformation, Godstow Nunnery, fortified during the Civil War, was accidentally razed by fire in 1645.

Sombre relics, exposed by the eroding waters, are occasionally glimpsed in the riverbank beside the ruined nunnery near the Trout Inn. A large stone coffin jutted out one day in 1944, and children rummaged through its occupant's remains. The bones belonged to an adult female, doubtless one of the nuns.

MYTHS AND MONSTERS

Hell Hounds

Benedict 'Old' Winchcombe of **Noke** was such a fanatical fan of hunting that not even death could stop him. The clamour of his eighteenth-century horses and hounds still haunts the village. He was so keen on hunting that he refused to cease even on Sunday, making it a seven-day chase. This kind of thing was never going to go down well with the local clergy, and when in the afterlife Old Winchcombe was still in hot pursuit of ghostly game, twelve parsons banded together to exorcise him.

Noke is on the fringes of Otmoor, which has a far older legend concerning the Gabriel Hounds: hunting dogs from Hell who ride howling through the storm-tossed skies, always on the lookout for a new leader of the pack. It seems that Old Winchcombe was given the role in the afterlife.

The Devil

One of the men who helped build the fourteenth-century churches at **Adderbury**, **Bloxham** and **King's Sutton**, never rested or accepted any payment. On one occasion, he slipped and dropped a huge load of mortar on Banbury, creating Crouch Hill. Only when the last tower was completed did the three brothers who had financed the church spree realise that they had been rubbing hods with the Devil, doing a spot of penance for some inscrutable mischief.

The Devil once manifested to members of the Hellfire Club at Oxford University in the eighteenth century, claiming at least one soul by pushing a man through a barred window on **Brasenose Lane**, like an egg through an egg-slice.

At **North Leigh**, a group of church truants were busy capturing badgers for a Sunday badger bait. Finding a particularly huge specimen, they eagerly stuffed it into their sack; but, when they opened it again, there was no animal within, just a hellish odour of brimstone.

One of the many entrances to Satan's kingdom can be found on the **Icknield Way** at **Swyncombe Downs**, just south of Britwell Salome. The Iron Age trench that runs along here is said to lead to the World's End, and onwards to Hell. A Watlington man put the theory to the test one day, walking for several hours and coming within sight of some fiery mountains. He could not proceed further on account of the sulphurous fumes.

Standing Stones

The large stones called the **Devil's Quoits** were, according to legend, erected by Satan in order to play a game of quoits, his opponent being a beggar, and the prize being the latter's soul. The game involves throwing horse-shoes (huge ones in this case), hoopla-like, at sticks. The Quoits can still be visited, just outside Stanton Harcourt. They fell, or were knocked over, many centuries ago, but were re-erected between 2002 and 2008, the surrounding earth enclosure being rebuilt at the same time.

Legend also associates the stones with a war, in which a captain called Harcourt was encouraged to turn the tide of battle after a rallying cry of: 'Stan' to un, Harcourt, stan' to un, Harcourt!' Harcourt won the battle, and the village has been called Stanton Harcourt ever since. Bullets used to be visible in the stones, mementoes of this legendary battle. In another version, Harcourt is described as 'Emperor of England', buried in the church with his sword, gun and military uniform. Yet another strand says the stones commemorate a Saxons versus Celts battle of AD 614.

The ruined Neolithic tomb called the **Hoar Stone**, in a small copse between Enstone and Fulwell, is said to be a petrified man, his dog and his horse. Every Midsummer's Eve (23 June) the man, sometimes known as the Old Soldier, goes to drink at a stream, either at Enstone or nearby Woodford. In other versions he is an ancient king, whose body was borne through the villages and interred here. Anyone who has attempted to relocate the stones in the past has been thwarted: they return to their original position when no one is looking. There is a tradition of a ghost too, emerging from the broken tomb.

The county's most famous ancient rocks are the **Rollright Stones** at Great Rollright on the Warwickshire border. They consist of a cluster of burial mound stones called the Whispering Knights, dating from around 4000 BC; a stone circle, the King's Men, erected 1,500 years later; and a monolith, the King's Stone, a mere youngster from 1500 BC.

The Rollright Stones are said to have been erected by Druids and are protected by fairies; bad luck will befall anyone tampering with them. But because folklore is nothing if not multi-headed and inconsistent, legend also claims that the stones are the petrified remains of a king and his knights.

The king, either a Briton or a Dane, was marching to war on the King of England, when he met a witch. She told him that as soon as he came within sight of the village of Long Compton (in Warwickshire), he would be guaranteed victory over the English. But the king never saw Long Compton: a hill sprang up and blocked the view, and he was turned to stone along with his handful of whispering knights.

A farmer later attempted to abduct one of the fossilised knights and use the monolith in his outhouse. He drove up the hill with four horses and a wagon, but the effort of bringing the stone downhill broke the cart and killed all four animals. The stone was successfully installed in the outhouse regardless; but bad luck came with it. His crops failed, his cattle died, his land had to be mortgaged, his possessions were all sold off, and in the end he was reduced to just one old horse and a broken-down cart.

Realising, a bit late in the day, that the stone was to blame, he decided to use the unpromising horse and cart combo to return the stone to its original setting at the top of the hill. The stone practically walked to the cart, the load was delivered, and the horse was as sprightly as a beast ten years younger. With the knight stone back in place, the farmer's fortunes improved.

Fairies

In 1010, the Vikings raped and pillaged their way through Oxfordshire. They burnt down Oxford and built entrenchments below the burial mound on the crown of the 148m-high Adwell Cop, near the village of Adwell. The mound was the site of otherworldly revelries (which is very hard to say after sampling the refreshments at such a revelry), with fairy dancers often sighted. At one point in the nineteenth century they were overheard singing, rather cryptically:

> At Adwell Cop there stands a cup.
> Drink the drink and eat the sop,
> And set the cup on Adwell Cop.

The burning of Oxford in 1010 is historical, but the entrenchments were nothing to do with the Vikings, the whole site dating from the Iron Age. The bit about the fairies is absolutely true, though. They inhabit old burial mounds and barrows, and like to dance on the top of them at Midsummer. The dozens of local hotspots include Brightwell Barrow at Wittenham Clumps; Churn Farm Barrow Cemetery near Blewbury; and, the biggest and best, Wayland's Smithy near Compton Beauchamp.

Giants

Robert Plot, first keeper of the Ashmolean Museum in the seventeenth century, believed that giants had once stalked the Oxfordshire countryside. He reached this conclusion after discovering an enormous thigh bone at Cornwell (which we now know to have belonged to the dinosaur Megalosaurus).

Modern giants were less impressive, though. 'The tallest that I have yet seen in our days was ... shewn publicly here at Oxford, seven foot and a half high,' he confessed. Such individuals turned up regularly at the city's St Giles' Fair over the next 250 years. Plot had, however, heard reports of contemporary men up to 12ft tall elsewhere in the world.

Shotover Forest used to have a resident giant, who threw, or 'shot over', various projectiles. The round stones found in the local sand are said to be his marbles. The giant was buried in an ancient barrow, 'The Giant's Grave', that sat on the hilltop until destroyed by tanks practising for some real shooting in the Second World War. In the seventeenth century, a picture of the giant was scratched into the red soil of the hill, wielding bow and arrow; but by 1763 it had disappeared.

Mermaids

In the 1820s, Charles Telfair of Mauritius sent John Shute Duncan, curator of the Ashmolean Museum, the head and forearms of a mermaid. It had, asserted Telfair, been caught near Mombasa. Duncan was unable to find anyone who had actually seen the creature while it was still alive, however; and the absence of the tail-end would seem to be an important omission.

Mermaids were a common feature of travelling fairs, and Oxford's annual St Giles' Fair in September regularly exhibited the creatures in the nineteenth and twentieth centuries. They were usually a sewn-together combination of monkey and cod: such was the 'South Sea mermaid' advertised in 1885. In 1886, a stuffed specimen (probably the same one) was billed as 'part woman part fish'; there was a 'Japanese mermaid' in 1891; and in the shadier booths you might glimpse a live woman with a discretely long wig and fishtail stockings.

Oxford used to have a Mermaid Tavern at the corner of Carfax. In the mid-seventeenth century, proprietor Anthony Hall issued trading tokens (a common practice for businesses between 1648 and 1672, when no copper coins were issued) sporting the image of a mermaid, and beer bottles with the same motif. Some examples can be seen in the Museum of Oxford. Burford, meanwhile, still has a thriving Mermaid Inn, its sign being the classic long-haired narcissistic fish-girl posing on a rock with a mirror.

Magdalen College has the prettiest of the species, flashing her tail flukes amongst the wonderful late twentieth-century stone corbels that decorate the edifice. She can be seen on the west tower and is said to have the face of a maid from the College buttery, whose looks enchanted the stonemason. Which is very much in the mermaid tradition. Seeing one, in folklore, usually leads to madness or death, a theme as ancient as the Sirens in Homer's *Odyssey*.

Unicorns

One of the pre-College University halls in Oxford was called Unicorn, probably after a coat of arms rather than a relic. The unicorn symbol survives in the heraldic arms of St Hilda's College, founded in 1893.

In 1458 a unicorn horn was given to New College, on condition that perpetual prayers should be sung in the College chapel for the safe transit of the giver's soul in the afterlife. The horn (a narwhal's) is still in the College's lumber room somewhere, one of two. A small section is missing: it was given grudgingly to the demanding Earl of Leicester in the sixteenth century, when he learnt of the horn's folkloric powers as an antidote to poison.

The Anatomy School at Christ Church had a unicorn horn too, whereas the Ashmolean could only boast a *Unicornu marinum*, or 'sea-unicorn' horn – i.e. the long, spiral tooth of a narwhal – which was very much second best to the terrestrial variety. A unicorn also graces the fifteenth-century stone fresco over the entrance to Merton College on Merton Street. But the Ashmolean has the best of them all – a 1481 ink drawing by Leonardo da Vinci, *A Unicorn Dipping its Horn into a Pool of Water*.

As Lewis Carroll writes in *Through the Looking Glass*, when Alice has expressed surprise at the appearance of the mythical beast:

> 'Well, now that we have seen each other...,' said the Unicorn, 'If you'll believe in me, I'll believe in you.'

Dragons

In the first century AD King Lud, in a bid to catch two destructive dragons, dug a pit in Oxford. He placed a bowl of mead in the pit and covered it with a silk sheet. The dragons were drawn to the mead and got tangled up in the silk. Safely wrapped up in a drunken stupor, they were buried under Mount Snowdon.

In the early 1700s, Jacob Bobart the Younger, keeper of Oxford's Botanical Gardens, shocked Oxford by producing the dried corpse of a small dragon. Scientists and poets poured forth their astonishment and admiration, at which point Bobart confessed that his dragon was actually the corpse of a rat, its sides stretched with sticks to resemble wings.

The carved Story Tree at Bury Knowle Park in Headington depicts characters from Middle Earth and Narnia, including Tolkien's dragon Smaug from *The Hobbit*.

I DON'T BELIEVE IT...

No snakes

First keeper of the Ashmolean Museum, Robert Plot, confirmed that there were no snakes in the north of the county:

In the Lordship of Blechington, and all the more Northern parts of Oxfordshire, no Snakes have been ever or very rarely seen, in so much that I met with several ancient people about Deddington and Banbury that scarce ever saw a Snake in their Lives ... And at Blechington 'twas confidently believed that a snake brought from any other place, and put down there, would instantly dye, till I made the Experiment and found no such matter: Whereupon I got leave ... to inclose my Snake ... to see what time would produce, leaving the Gardener in trust to observe it strictly, who found it indeed, after three weeks time, dead, without any sensible external hurt.

Angels of the Earth

One November in the late nineteenth century, eighty-five-year-old Mrs Wain of Adderbury told a friend with great confidence that the prevailing cold winds would continue for three more months. When asked how she could be so certain, Mrs Wain explained that on Martinmas Eve (10 November), between 11 p.m. and midnight, the four Angels of the Earth exercise their wings by whizzing around the earth. Whichever direction their feather-powered draughts are coming from as the clock strikes midnight will dictate the prevailing wind, and all its attendant weather, for the following three months.

Mrs Wain had received the divine weatherlore from her father, a man who went by the angelic name of Messenger. Every Martinmas Eve, just before 11 p.m., Messenger and some faithful companions used to walk to the ironstone pits near Adderbury Park and spend an hour listening and watching for windy clues. He never actually saw the four Angels of the Earth, but told his daughter that he heard them fanning the skies. In the last few minutes of the vigil the winds seemed to do battle, before settling down and fixing on one direction at midnight.

Stealing breeches

Maid servants in the Launton and Bicester region used to ask their male colleagues for ivy to decorate the house at Christmas. If the man failed to bring the greenery, the maid was entitled to steal a pair of his breeches and nail them to a gate, preferably one facing the road. This custom was discontinued in the early eighteenth century. Twenty-first-century maids could pinch the men's mobile phones from their breeches and send rude messages to everyone in their contacts list instead.

Moreton

According to the anonymous 1537 play *Thersites*, the village of Moreton can be invoked in a tongue-twister, the successful completion of which will expel intestinal parasites. The unlikely cure runs:

> The mawe of the morecocke that made Mawd to mowe,
> When Martylmas at Moreton morened for the snowe.

(The maw of the moorcock which made Maud mock,
When Martinmas at Moreton mourned for the snow.)

Voodoo

In June 1954, near the River Evenlode at Combe, a fisherman discovered a small puppet hanging by a grass noose from a dead willow tree. The arms and head were made from twisted-up sections of the *Illustrated London News*. Delicate dissection of the straw body revealed the cast skin of a capsid bug nymph. The folklorist who investigated, H.A. Beecham, sniffed witchery, perhaps of the voodoo-doll kind.

But the only folkloric parallel he could unearth was a story by M.R. James in *More Ghost Stories of an Antiquary* (1911). Speaking of an ancient gallows tree, James' narrator says:

> ... at certain times of the year it was the custom for those that wished to secure a successful issue to their affairs, whether of love or the ordinary business of life, to suspend from its boughs small images or puppets rudely fashioned of straw, twigs, or the like rustic materials.

King's Evil

By the seventeenth century, kings and queens no longer felt at ease with the 'Laying on of Hands' ceremony, once believed to cure scrofula (or 'King's Evil'). But simple country folk were still keen to give the alternative medicine a go. Disapproving Charles II drew up legislation requiring would-be patients to bring a certificate from their parish priests, confirming that they had not been groped by the anti-scrofulous royal hands already. This was in addition to an earlier law limiting the times of the year when the treatment was available.

This is the origin of entries in the parish register at Waterperry for 1684 and 1708, declaring that named local sufferers were eligible for the royal hands. 1708 was very late in the day for the treatment: Queen Anne, who died in 1714, brought an end to the touchy-feely nonsense.

Dead Man's Hand

It was a widely believed that a dead person's hand could cure warts, birthmarks and cysts. Nurses would often take children to receive the laying on of cold hands, which was said to be much more effective than the alternative cures of licking the spots daily or rubbing them with a potato. Any dead body would suffice, from poor old granny to the local mass murderer. But a man who died a violent death was best, and victims of the gallows were the favourite source.

Touching the afflicted area (nine strokes was the recommended dose) tied the fate of the blemish to the dead body part, and, as the latter decayed, so would the former diminish. This macabre medicine was still being used in the mid-nineteenth century, and it is said that its demise was not due to a lessening of faith in the cure, but to the higher fees being demanded by the hangman.

Thunder and lightning

In 1928, a red-streaked celt – a stone believed to be a thunderbolt – was shipped from a site near Bhandari in India to the Pitt Rivers Museum in Oxford. Its native owner claimed that it was still 'live' and had caused much damage, including a lightning strike which had destroyed his house. He had picked it up as a lucky talisman, but was now keen to part with it.

The man who relieved him of the burden, Mr C.W. Pawsey, warned Dr Hutton at the museum that he had 'better dispose of the celt quickly, unless you want a new bungalow!' It was duly installed, but was, indeed, still fizzing. In November 1928 a great storm blew away a large portion of the Pitt Rivers roof, and only the cold logic of a scientist would claim that the cause was anything other than the stone thunderbolt from the stormy Naga Hills.

GRAVE NEWS

Captain Hampden Pye

At midnight on 23 June, the headless ghost of Captain Hampden Pye walks by the wall of All Saints' Church in Faringdon. At his mother's insistence, Pye had fought against the Spanish in 1702 in an army led by Sir George Rooke. This had been to separate him from his intended bride, who was deemed to be way below Pye's social station. The lovelorn lad was decapitated in an explosion on the battlefield, and his ghost returned home to make a Pye-in-the-sky tryst with his beloved.

In an alternative version it is said that Pye was unfaithful to his wife, who showed her disapproval by blasting his head off with a gun. The spirit was laid to rest by an exorcist a few years after his death.

Francis Page

Steeple Aston church has a stone memorial to 'Hanging Judge' Francis Page. It is said that the widows of the 100 men he condemned to death exact an unorthodox form of revenge every Midsummer's Eve. They attack his restless spirit on the pond at Steeple Aston, where it bobs up and down inside a beer barrel; and, to make it even weirder, they do this in the form of owls.

Page was famously mean, as well as bloodthirsty. He refused to pay the stonemason who had worked on the Page family memorial in the church, due to the fact that he had neglected to carve the wedding ring on the finger of Page's otherwise carefully chiselled wife.

Claude Duval

The Holt Hotel at Hopcrofts Holt near Steeple Aston has the honour of being haunted by the French 'gentleman highwayman' Claude Duval. He stayed in the fifteenth-century coaching inn on numerous occasions in the mid-seventeenth century, and stalks the site in the afterlife (even though the present structure dates from 1800). Room 3 is said to be a favourite haunt.

In life, Duval's most famous (and probably apocryphal) exploit was a robbery in which he agreed to take only half the loot if his victim's wife danced with him, which of course she did. He was hanged at Tyburn in London, aged twenty-six, in 1670, and the inscription on his grave at St Paul's Church in Covent Garden used to read:

> Here lies DuVall: Reder, if male thou art,
> Look to thy purse; if female, to thy heart.

Empress Matilda

Empress Matilda, denied the crown of England by her cousin King Stephen in the twelfth century, was imprisoned at Oxford Castle. She has haunted it ever since, and was the most frequently identified ghost in Britain between 2007 and 2009, managing thirty-two manifestations. Quite how ghost-spotters knew they were looking at Matilda is a moot point.

Oxford Castle.

Amy Robsart

On 8 September 1560 Amy Robsart, wife of Elizabeth I's court favourite Robert Dudley, took a tumble down the stairs at Cumnor Place. It was widely rumoured that she had been murdered, and wounds to the head in addition to her broken neck seemed to back this up. The Queen had fallen in love with Dudley, and was said to want him as her husband.

Robert Dudley was believed to have arranged Robsart's murder, in spite of the official verdict of accidental death. Walter Scott fanned the flames by casting her as his tragic, murdered heroine in *Kenilworth* (1821).

Amy was buried at St Mary's Cathedral in Oxford, but her ghost lingered at Cumnor Place. It was a noisy and fearsome spirit, warranting the intervention of nine Oxford exorcists in the eighteenth century. They managed to 'lay' the ghost in the church pond at Cumnor, and, although silent from then on, the hot-headed phantom prevented the water there from freezing ever again.

Cumnor Place was rented out by its eighteenth-century owners – on account of the ghost, according to legend. The building eventually succumbed to ruin in 1810; but villagers were still spotting Amy's ghost in the twentieth century, and she is also said to haunt Cornbury Park near Charlbury. Spotting her here is a portent of doom. Robert Dudley is said to have spied her at Cornbury and died ten days later.

White horse

Cornbury Park is the family home of Lord and Lady Rotherwick, set in a 700-acre private estate of ancient forest and parkland. It started life as a royal hunting lodge, attached to Wychwood Forest, and continues its involvement with ancient rural ways by running bushcraft courses (i.e. the stuff any self-respecting peasant would have known in previous centuries) and hosting a livery stable.

One spirited former inhabitant of the stables might still be roaming free. A ghostly, riderless, white (sometimes grey) stallion is at times seen galloping around the Charlbury neighbourhood and jumping over hedges.

William Field

When, some time around 1850, John and James Parkes of South Moreton heard that eleven clergymen had been summoned to exorcise a tricky ghost, they were keen to get front-row seats. They hid under the straw in the barn where the exorcism was to take place, and waited, quiet as mice.

The ghost was that of farmer William Field, who had hanged himself in the barn in 1804 and subsequently haunted the yard outside. When his summoned spirit appeared, it asked the clerics whether they would hand over the two mice who were hiding under the straw, or the cock on the dunghill. To the relief of the Parkes brothers the clerics offered the fowl, which promptly exploded. The wraith was successfully 'laid' in a nearby pond, with a stake hammered through it like a TV vampire.

Grey Lady

Sixteenth-century Horspath Manor is haunted by a Grey Lady, the wraith of a woman killed by her husband during an argument. After the murder he stuffed her down a 'priest hole', a hidden room used by recusants (those who refused to accept the Protestant religion) for concealing Catholic priests. The Grey Lady has been seen many times – most famously in 1878, when a man fired his gun at her three times but only found two of his bullets afterwards, embedded in the wall.

George Cobb

Adderbury used to have a large residence called Cobb House, occupied by George Cobb. Fond of four old oak trees on his land, he ordered on his deathbed that they should never be felled. But his successors ignored him and cut down the trees, prompting Cobb's ghost to haunt the village in a funeral coach.

William Wilcote and Elizabeth Blacket

Sir William Wilcote and his wife Lady Elizabeth Blacket used to haunt the vicinity of Wilcote, until successfully exorcised. Their mid-fifteenth-century tombs are in a chantry constructed in North Leigh church by Lady Blacket, and the accompanying effigies of the couple used to lie with their elbows close together, according to legend.

As time passes the stone arms drift further apart, and it is said that when the distance becomes too great, Lady Blacket will return from the grave to haunt the village.

It seems that simple practicalities lie behind the legend: William's effigy was moved sideways to accommodate Elizabeth's after she joined him in the afterlife.

Ghostly monk

Between Chesterton and Weston-on-the-Green, the ghost of a monk lurks. In life he had an affair with a woman called Mad Maude of Weston, and his randy ghost chases anyone it meets. Maude herself haunts Weston Manor Hotel, on the site of a former nunnery, in Weston-on-the-Green.

Mrs Whittaker

A woman called Whittaker from Bampton Manor died of a broken heart when her husband took a lover. Her angry spirit was laid by exorcists in a local pond; but when it dried up Mrs Whittaker returned, more terrifying than ever. She was laid again by a posse of exorcists, in a barrel of strong beer, and walled up in the cellar at the manor.

Mrs Hall?

A similar tale is told of a woman who drowned herself in a pond at the back of Stanton Harcourt Manor House. Whenever the pond dried up she was said to walk, or to drive in a coach-and-four. She was eventually laid in the pond a second time by some parsons, and villagers ensured that the pond never dried up again. In some versions she is named as Mrs Hall, who poisoned herself when her husband took a lover at the local inn.

Lady Alice Harcourt

In yet another version of this legend, the Stanton ghost is named as Lady Alice Harcourt. She was murdered at the manor and thrown from a window in Pope's Tower, part of the fifteenth-century private chapel in the manor grounds. It was named after eighteenth-century poet and frequent visitor Alexander Pope, who

Pope's Tower.

complicated the legends further by referring to a 'Lady Frances', who haunted a walled-up room in the tower.

Hanged boy
The Old Gaol in Abingdon, built by Napoleonic prisoners of war in 1811, was a sports centre in the 1970s, and was redeveloped as luxury flats, shops and cafés in 2011. Its most disturbing ghost was that of an eight-year-old boy, hanged in the mid-nineteenth century after torching a couple of barns, and the youngest person in the country to receive that penalty. His ghost was frequently spotted prior to the '70s makeover.

Longueville brothers
In 1712, a family called Longueville rented the manor house at Fritwell. Two brothers of the family fell out over a girl, the youngest imprisoning the elder in the manor's 'priest hole'. The victim died of starvation after fourteen years in what was described as 'a human kennel', and has haunted as 'a frightful apparition' ever since.

George Napier
Jesuit priest George Napier was hanged, drawn and quartered at Oxford during the reign of Queen Elizabeth I, and the various chunks of cadaver were placed in different bits of the city. Returning from the realm of the dead, Napier attempted to round up his body parts. He managed to find everything apart from his head, and he can still be seen on Banbury Road, where it was last sighted.

Haunted wardrobe
The Narnia wardrobe is not the only uncanny bedroom furniture in the county. In 1937 a wardrobe terrorised a bedroom in Carterton Manor, opening and slamming in spite of efforts to tie the doors shut. When the ghost of an old man in a deerstalker hat materialised, the owner decided to rid herself of the nuisance in a most English manner – putting an ad in the local paper requesting removal men.

Kassam Stadium
In 2001, Revd Richard Harries, Bishop of Oxford, was summoned to Kassam Stadium football ground in Cowley, Oxford, to exorcise it. Superstitious fans claimed that a malicious Roma man, evicted from the site when the stadium was being built, had cursed the whole enterprise. The ceremony was carried out, even though no ghost had ever been seen or poltergeist heard. The problem was simply an invisible malicious force – a good enough definition of a curse, and

surely the best excuse ever for a football team's poor performance. Oxford United had, indeed, managed thirteen defeats in their seventeen games during 2001.

Roland Jenks

This was nowhere near as effective as the curse placed on Oxford in 1577 by Roland Jenks. Convicted of supporting the Pope by producing illicit Catholic books, he was sentenced to be nailed by the ears to the castle pillory. When he managed to tear himself away, he cursed the court that had condemned him: a few days later two judges, the coroner and several jurors from his trial were dead from typhus, along with others to the total of 300.

GHOSTLY ONE-LINERS

In the Thames, by Abingdon Bridge, the apparition of a female's head and arms – presumably attached to a ghostly body beneath the water – is seen floating by.

The hated Lord of Burford Manor, Sir Lawrence Tanfield (1551–1625), and his wife race around the town in a fiery coach: to view them spells death and disaster.

On a similar theme, Sandford-on-Thames suffers the attentions of a headless horseman and his coach-and-four, racing through fields near the village every Christmas Eve.

Boudicca's Iceni charioteers can be seen dashing down the Icknield Way near Watlington, en route to the sacking of St Albans in AD 61; and her enemies, a Roman legion, are sometimes spotted too.

The Old Rectory in Burford is haunted by a bell, ringing at 2 a.m. from no known source – although an Augustinian monk who haunts the spot with an anachronistic gun may be responsible.

Somewhere on the Burford to Minster Lovell road lurks a supernatural cloud, roaming the thoroughfare with a mind of its own: if it envelops you, let the terror ensue.

The Elizabethan Mapledurham House is haunted by two ghosts: a servant who was killed by his master, and the murderer, dragging the corpse across the floor.

Sarah Fletcher, of Courtiers House in Clifton Hampden, had an unfaithful husband and hanged herself from her four-poster bed in a fit of depression in 1854: she has haunted the house ever since, dressed in sombre black with a purple ribbon in her hair.

The ghost of Archbishop Laud, beheaded in 1645 and buried beneath the altar in the chapel at St John's College, Oxford, walks on air above the ground, presumably at the original floor level; and as a party piece he bowls his head across the floor at anyone who makes a Laudable effort to resemble a skittle.

Many Oxford Colleges have resident ghosts, including:

Exeter: the headless John Crocker, Elizabethan scholar, dressed in yellow jacket, gown and breeches.

Magdalen: a headless black-clad monk, plus disembodied footsteps and other noises.

Merton: Colonel Francis Windebank, shot in the Fellows Garden by Oliver Cromwell after surrendering to him in 1645.

The tweedy, waistcoated, pipe-smoking ghost of J.R.R. Tolkien is occasionally spotted in the precincts of Merton College; and later occupants of his study have reported the smell of tobacco, as if its pipe-loving occupant had vacated the premises moments before.

University: Obadiah Walker, Master of the College in the 1680s, lingers in Room 1 on Staircase 8 in the Front Quad.

Queen's: Cuthbert Shields, a clergyman who believed himself the reincarnation of St Cuthbert, left his archive to the College, stating that it was not to be opened for fifty years: the papers were finally unboxed in the 1950s, and since then Shields has haunted the upper library.

Magdalen Tower.

7

THE WORKING LIFE

GRIEVANCES IN THE WORKPLACE

The bulk of the population in modern Oxfordshire's villages pursue work and lifestyles that would have been as alien to the nineteenth-century residents of those same villages as a commune of vegetarian Martians. Much of the rural workforce was abandoning the land in the later Victorian period, complaining of intolerable rural conditions. The Liberal Party heard Oxfordshire delegates voice their concerns at a Reform Conference in London, 1891:

'I was in a house in Oxfordshire, at Tackley, the other night, where the drain actually ran right under the floor. Just a week ago, the cesspool overflowed into the well, and that is the stuff that they have to drink ... I am sorry to tell you that is the position of things in scores of agricultural villages, where the stuff out of the farmers' middens runs near or into the well where the people have to drink.'

'A man gets taken on by a farmer, and just because he will not put up with all the tyranny imaginable he is sacked. The next week, if he does not get out of the house, his things are put outside on the road.'

'In some villages you will find that the majority of the allotments belong to the parson ... When the farmers had the ground before, it was ... about 13 shillings an acre; the parson, in his benevolence, raises it to about 52 shillings an acre ... This is the man who says "Dearly beloved brethren" on Sundays!'

Charterville Allotments
The Charterville Allotments in Minster Lovell were established by the Chartist National Land Company in 1847 as a means of bestowing small-scale land ownership. There were eighty smallholdings across 300 acres, complete with cottages and a share of forty oxen, eighteen pigs, manure, firewood and seed.

This was a means of gaining a political voice: only male landowners were entitled to vote in elections at that time. But the NLC was scuppered by far more powerful landowners, who subjected it to the scrutiny of a Select Committee. The lottery system of allocating the land was outlawed, the company was wound up by Act of Parliament in 1851, and the plots had to be allocated via auction. In other words, the poor shareholders of the defunct NLC, the sole reason for the establishment of the Allotments, couldn't afford to take part.

The original Chartist plots survive as an area of neat bungalows with large gardens in the New Minster area of the village.

Lace-making
Lace-making employed thousands of women and children in the Bicester area during the nineteenth century. In 1859, a damning report on the industry concluded: 'All accounts agree in representing the occupation of lace-making in these districts as highly injurious to those engaged in it.'

Consumption and dyspepsia killed many lace-makers, mainly girls, some as young as four. Stunted growth resulted from the cramped conditions of their twelve-plus hour shifts, with no exercise or fresh air: it was said that you could tell a lace-maker from her walk. Other physical conditions noted were scrofula, indigestion, distortion of the spine, and poor eyesight sometimes leading to blindness. For older females, difficult labours, miscarriages and 'derangement of the uterine functions' were said to be 'almost universal'.

John Ruskin
John Ruskin, first Slade Professor of Fine Art at Oxford University, art critic, Christian socialist and philanthropist, was very fond of North Hinksey (east Oxford) and is commemorated with a Blue Plaque on one of the former village's cottage walls. In 1874, Ruskin decided to build a road across the boggy ground here. The initiative, he thought, would benefit not just the locals, but the Oxford University students he roped in as labourers.

The students started work on the new road, bordering it with banks of flowers. Among the navvies was Oscar Wilde, engaging in his first, but sadly not last, bout of hard labour. Wilde recalled the unorthodox month's work, its high hopes and ultimate failure, in an essay published in 1879. He explains that Ruskin thought 'wrong that all the best physique and strength of the young men in England should be spent aimlessly on cricket ground or river'. He thought men should work at something beneficial to society, 'something by which we might show that in all labour there was something noble.'

Wilde goes on: 'Ruskin worked with us in the mist and rain and mud of an Oxford winter, and our friends and our enemies came out and mocked us from the bank. We did not mind it much then, and we did not mind it afterwards at all, but worked away for two months at our road. And what became of the road? Well, like a bad lecture it ended abruptly – in the middle of the swamp. Ruskin going away to Venice, when we came back for the next term there was no leader, and the "diggers", as they called us, fell asunder.'

Ruskin College in Oxford is named after the great man. *War and Peace* author Leo Tolstoy described him as 'one of the most remarkable men not only of England and of our generation, but of all countries and times'.

Oxfam

The embryonic Oxford Committee for Famine Relief (Oxfam) held its first public meeting in the library of the Church of St Mary the Virgin in Oxford in 1942. The organisers, all Quakers, were concerned that the British Government's policy of banning food exports to German-controlled mainland Europe was harming civilians. The Oxford Committee, along with other pressure groups, urged the Government to allow controlled food distribution under the guiding hand of the International Red Cross – their specific concern being occupied Greece, where people were dying in their thousands through starvation. The aid got through.

After the war, Oxfam continued to organise collections of food and clothing. By the late 1950s it was active in most of the poorer parts of the world. The headquarters of Oxfam GB are still in Oxford, at Cowley, and employ more than 6,000 people worldwide.

A Blue Plaque at 17 Broad Street, Oxford, commemorates Oxfam founder and first Honorary Secretary Cecil Jackson-Cole (1901–79). A plaque in St Mary's commemorates the inaugural meeting.

INDUSTRY

Wool

In the Middle Ages, when wool and woollen products were England's chief industry, Witney's 'broad cloth' and blankets (named after fourteenth-century Bristol merchant Thomas Blanket) were said to be the best, due to their unusual whiteness. Producers claimed the secret lay in the River Windrush, source of the water used in the manufacturing process.

The word 'blanket' was not limited to bed coverings: it covered all manner of heavy woollen cloth for furnishings and clothing. Witney Blankets did not have one specific style, but they were renowned for their thick, weatherproof 'pile'. In 1716, playwright and poet John Gay summed this up in his poem 'Trivia':

> True Witney Broad-cloth with its Shag unshorn,
> Unpierc'd is in the lashing Tempest worn.

In the nineteenth century, 'Witney' became a byword for quality, regardless of where the item was made. The situation was resolved in 1908, when a law stated that it could only be a 'Witney' if it was produced in the town. Cheddar, Melton Mowbray and Champagne, to name but three, have fought similar battles over the years.

In the 1950s, man-made fibres were in the ascendant, and a Witney, for the first time, did not necessarily have to be woollen. At the industry's height there were five blanket factories in Witney; but the last one, Early's, closed in 2002. The villains of the piece were those chill-banishing innovations, the duvet and central heating. Only echoes remain: Blanket Hall on the High Street, and the local football team's nickname The Blanketmen.

Oxfordshire's wool-based industry included plush or shag (the type of material most commonly seen these days on teddy bears and other 'plush' cuddly toys). Several villages around Banbury specialised in spinning the yarn, which was then sent to Banbury for dyeing and preparing for market. One of the spinning centres was Shutford, which maintained a toehold after the rise of Coventry and its power looms, unlike most other former strongholds of the ancient craft.

Shutford got its own power looms in 1885, surviving by concentrating on niche market high-quality plush for liveries, upholstery and furnishings. Such was its reputation that Nicholas II, the last Tsar of Russia, ordered Shutford plush for his coronation in 1896, having encountered it during his visit to England shortly before his accession. Unfortunately for the Tsar, the material was not bullet proof. He was killed in 1918. Shutford's plush industry died thirty years later.

There are many nineteenth-century weavers' cottages in Bloxham. The weaving industry resulted in rivalry between the various villages involved, giving rise to such doggerel as:

> Bloxham for length,
> Adderbury for strength,
> And King's Sutton for Beauty.

and:

> Bloxham dogs,
> Come to Adderbury to buy your togs!

Paper

Demolished in 2004, the paper mill on the Thames at Lower Wolvercote in suburban Oxford used to supply all the paper requirements of Oxford University Press, and of Jackson's Oxford Journal (published 1754–1928). Powered solely by the Thames until 1811, it then installed a steam engine requiring 100 tons of coal a week. The main purpose of the Oxford Canal was to transport such coal as this.

Wood pulp, and therefore paper, is absorbent. In manufacturing paper for printing and writing, cancelling this absorbent quality with a solution called 'size' is essential. In the late eighteenth century, a workman at East Hagbourne Mill (some versions of the story locate the paper mill at South Moreton) either omitted the size or spilled acid on the finished product. The outcome was the same: paper that soaked up ink like a sponge. In one simple error, blotting paper was invented and was soon being sold commercially by mill owner William Slade (1766–1801). Another version of the story says that the inventor was Slade's son John. He was born in 1797, running the mill from 1824 to 1845. The fact that blotting paper was available in the early nineteenth century undermines John's claim to the invention.

Gas Works

Before electricity, Oxford was noted for its Gas Works. Gas lights flared at stalls during the September St Giles' Fair, and lit many suburbs and alleyways.

Writing in 1828, Nathaniel Whittock enthused: 'The gas produced here is remarkably pure and brilliant; and by the judicious and liberal arrangement of the laws of the company, the lighting of the city in every part is considered of more importance than the accumulation of profit to the individuals; consequently the illumination of the city, during the winter months, is as brilliant as can be desired.'

Steel
Woodstock was once renowned for its polished steel, and the sole ingredient was said to be used horse-shoe nails. It was undercut by cheaper products from Birmingham in the nineteenth century.

Iron
During the Second World War, a 3.5-mile railway was built by German prisoners of war to link a series of ironstone quarries with the main line. This was the heyday of the Oxfordshire Ironstone Company, which operated between 1917 and 1978, quarrying one of the biggest orefields in the country. At its height it was churning out 40,000 tons of ore per week. But the boom came and went, and today the only functional expression of the old industry is the Ironstone Benefice. This is a group of churches lying along the old quarrying grounds, at Alkerton, Balscote, Drayton, Hanwell, Horley, Shenington and Wroxton.

Chinnor Cement and Lime Company
The Chinnor Cement and Lime Company's works at Chinnor dominated the skyline from 1908 until its demolition in 2011. The site has been redeveloped as a housing estate. Quarrying and cement-making ceased in 1989, bringing to an end a long history of industry in the village. Prior to cement, the area had produced lace (with 268 registered lace-makers in 1851), and housed several artisans involved in the furniture-making industry of High Wycombe.

None of which made Chinnor a rich place: prior to the twentieth century, the vicar of St Andrew's Church threw an annual dole of bread, cheese and beer from the tower to the poor masses below. This was transmuted to a more orthodox handout when brawling brought the tradition into disrepute. Blankets and clothes were sometimes doled out at Christmas too.

Didcot Power Station
Didcot Power Station produces enough electricity to satisfy the needs of three million users. It is made up of two separate stations, with Didcot A and its famous cooling towers due to close in 2015. It was designed in 1970 as a coal-burning plant, and was later converted to take gas and biomass such as wood shavings too. Its closure is part of the national – and indeed international – push to reduce carbon emissions. The demolition is no big deal for RWE npower, who run

the site, as they plan to build thirty new power stations across Europe over the next few years.

Didcot B, built in 1997 and producing a third of the station's overall output, is a far more efficient gas-burning plant, capturing twice as much heat from an equivalent amount of natural gas burnt at an older station such as Didcot A. Carbon emissions are still high of course, but lower than at many other power stations, and nitrous oxide emissions are relatively low too. None of which has prevented sustained criticism from Greenpeace.

Didcot Power Station was ranked number three in a survey on British eyesores in 2003. But what will the empty skyline do once those cooling towers have gone?

Harwell Laboratory

Prior to the twentieth century, Harwell was famous for one thing – cherry orchards. The rural idyll ended in 1937, when an airfield was built for launching glider-borne troops into Normandy for the abortive invasions of the Second World War. In 1946 the site became Harwell Laboratory, the base of the Atomic Energy Research Establishment, the UK HQ for nuclear power research. Europe's first ever nuclear reactor was built here in 1946, one of five that have occupied the site.

Harwell Laboratory's most infamous occupant was Klaus Fuchs, a German communist who had fled from the Nazis. In 1946 he was made first Head of the Theoretical Physics Division at Harwell, but soon fell under suspicion. A joint British and US intelligence operation, called the Venona Project, had cracked a code through which agents like Fuchs had been communicating nuclear secrets to the Soviets.

In January 1950, Fuchs confessed to MI5 that he was a spy, and was sentenced to fifteen years in prison. The Soviets, allies at this point in history, denied that Fuchs was working for them. He was released from Wakefield Prison after nine years, and lived and worked in communist East Germany until his death in 1988. Upon retirement in 1979, he was awarded the Order of Merit for the Fatherland and the Order of Karl Marx.

Harwell Science and Innovation Campus currently occupies the old airfield, employing some 4,500 people in 150 different onsite organisations. The nuclear reactors have all been shut down, the remaining three structures due to be decommissioned (i.e. demolished) by 2022. Time for those cherry trees once again …

Motors

William Morris, owner of Morris Motors and creator of 'affordable motoring', was born in 1877 in a terraced house at Cowley near Oxford. These Everyman beginnings never entirely left him, even when untold wealth had removed him several strata, socially, from his modest beginnings. In spite of his philanthropic instincts he was, by all accounts, neither warm nor charismatic, just endlessly practical.

His business breakthrough came at the age of sixteen, with a bicycle repair business in the shed at the bottom of the family garden. Having shifted from bikes to cars, he designed his first commercial model, the Morris Oxford (aka the Bullnose Morris), in 1912, moving the workshop to a disused military training college in Cowley soon after. The 'affordable motoring' concept literally changed the nature of Britain's roads, bringing motor vehicles within reach of a broad cross section of the population.

During the First World War the Cowley works produced munitions, and manufactured Spitfires and Tiger Moths in the Second bout. Morris was knighted in 1929, and became Lord Nuffield in 1934. In the preceding year he had moved to Nuffield Place near Henley-on-Thames, inspiring his chosen title.

By 1937, Morris Motors Ltd was the largest motor manufacturer in Europe. Morris founded Nuffield College in that year, though it was not completed until 1960 due to building restrictions during the post-war rearmament drive. In 1943 the Nuffield Foundation was launched with a kick-start of £10 million. Indeed, it is said that William Morris gave away the equivalent in today's money of £11 billion. He died in 1963.

BMW owns the Cowley site these days, producing the iconic Mini.

The motor industry has other Oxfordshire links. MG cars used to be produced in Abingdon: the factory closed in 1980 after fifty-one years, and all that remains today is the headquarters of the thriving MG Car Club.

Wykham Mill in Bloxham was once a king of the road too, producing vehicles such as the Jaguar XJ220 super car and the Aston Martin DB7. The factory closed in 2004.

Formula One is still parked locally. Virgin F1 has its technical base in Bicester; and Lotus Renault F1 has its chassis designed and built at Enstone, with the car engines coming from Viry-Châtillon near Paris.

F1 teams liaise closely with Oxford Brookes School of Technology which, along with Oxford and Cranfield Universities, is also part of Faraday Advance. This takes an innovative, scientific look at future technology, looking for an equal ratio of low-pollution to high-efficiency in all forms of transport.

Bloxham's Wykham Mill is now occupied by Vantage Business Park, named after the last Aston Martin produced here, the DB7 V12 Vantage. The headline in the *Banbury Guardian*, 5 December 2003, which foreshadowed the car plant's closure, announced 'End of the line for 007's super car'.

But the real 'super car' is the one being fitted out by Oxford Yasa Motors. The company has developed engines for high performance electronic vehicles, and Yasa is also leading the way in the post-fossil fuel aerospace and industrial sectors. The pro-petrol lobby, still chuckling at memories of wobbly Sinclair C5s, needs to digest the implications of the YASA-750 electric motor: it accelerates from 0-60 in three seconds and has a top speed of 140mph.

Biomass

Nestling on the edge of Kingston Blount near Thame is the controversial C.J. Day Associates, a firm of engineers who advise on, and build, biomass power plants. The controversy lies in the fact that not everyone thinks biomass fuels (plants and wood grown for burning or for the production of ethanol fuel, and landfill-derived methane gas) are The Way Forward. Much of the protesting over proposed power plants is directed at disruption and eyesores rather than the nature of the technology itself.

But biomass-derived power is carbon-neutral, and advocates also point out that it comes with far less pollution risk than nuclear power, the other big alternative to coal and gas. The 'carbon-neutral' asset is explained by the fact that the gas released is already part of earth's current carbon cycle, as opposed to fossil fuels that release carbon that has been locked out of the cycle for millions of years.

WATERWAYS

Isis

The River Thames' alternative name in Oxford is the Isis, usually applied only to that section that flows through the city. The name is still used by the Ordnance Survey, however, for the stretch between Oxford and Dorchester-on-Thames.

In the seventeenth century, goods shipped from London to Oxford via the Thames had to stop at Burcot. The river was unnavigable beyond the village, and the barges had to unload their cargoes onto wagons for the rest of the journey.

The first attempt to solve this problem came in 1605, with the formation of the Oxford-Burcot Commission. After a faltering start, in 1623 the Commission was granted the power to tax Oxford's University and city to finance its work, and it was soon cleaning the river of sediment and accumulated sewage, and installing the locks and weirs necessary to admit traffic. In 1631, locks at Iffley, Sandford and Swift Ditch (near the present Abingdon Lock) were constructed, and in 1635 a barge finally made it through to Oxford.

Lock at Iffley.

The initiative was expanded in 1751 with the establishment of the Thames Navigation Commissioners, with jurisdiction over the whole river as far as Staines.

Oxford Canal

The Oxford Canal links the city via Banbury with Coventry and Rugby, taking in some of the best countryside in Oxfordshire, Northamptonshire and Warwickshire. The canal owes its conception to an Act of Parliament in 1769, which allowed a waterway that would link London to the industrial Midlands for trade purposes. The initial survey was masterminded by waterway engineer extraordinaire James Brindley and his brother-in-law Samuel Simcock, who completed the job when Brindley died in 1772.

The final stretch to Oxford was not completed until 1790, following a second Act to raise more funds. For all its ingenious beauty, much of the canal was built as cheaply as possible: single gates on the locks instead of double ones; lift or swing-bridges instead of sturdier, more expensive brick ones; and the use of the existing River Cherwell at Shipton-on-Cherwell instead of cutting a new canal. This stretch still causes difficulties for boaters. The canal also uses twists and turns to get round hills (a so-called 'contour canal') rather then having purpose-built tunnels or aqueducts. Some of these contours were ironed out in the 1820s, but many remain.

The Oxford Canal's heyday was brief: between 1790 and 1805 it carried all water traffic between London and the Midlands. But then the Grand Junction Canal opened, and much of the London traffic chose this new, more direct route. The one section that remained busy was between Napton and Braunston, which formed a link between the Warwick & Napton Canal and the Grand Junction. The Oxford Canal Company had opposed the new route, of course, and the Act which allowed the competition to go ahead included a clause by which Grand Junction paid Oxford 'bar tolls' as a form of compensation for the loss of traffic.

The canal's '11-mile pound' is a twisting stretch that takes 11 miles to cover 5 miles as-the-crow-flies. Tooley's Boatyard is another landmark, a boatyard-cum-museum now listed as an Ancient Monument. It features in Tom Rolt's canalside classic *Narrow Boat* (1944, and still in print), which has since become synonymous with the boatyard. A bridge over the canal in Banbury was named the Tom Rolt in 1999, and a Blue Plaque was placed on Tooley's in 2010 to mark the centenary of Rolt's birth.

Horse traction was used on the Oxford Canal long after it had been superseded by coal and diesel. The last animal-powered barge retired in 1959. It had been drawn by a mule and was the last horse-drawn freight narrowboat in Britain.

SOME UNUSUAL TRADES

Beckley Foundation

The Beckley Foundation, a charitable trust based in the grounds of the Tudor edifice Beckley Park, is unique. Its mission is to get to grips with the concept and various practical, moral and philosophical implications of consciousness, and observe how this is affected by various states, such as meditation, old age and psychoactive substances. To their supporters they are a scientific melting pot, whose goal is a deeper understanding of how humans function; to opponents they are amoral magic-mushroom-munching hippies undermining hardline drugs policy.

The Foundation does not hide from the more controversial aspects of its work, and one of its missions is to 'change global drugs policy to reflect a more rational, evidence-based approach, shifting the emphasis from criminalisation to health'. They oppose the global 'war on drugs', arguing that the current approach is not working but merely feeding a Prohibition Era-style racket of black market atrocities and human misery. They also seek to increase our understanding of what various illegal substances actually do – physically, socially and economically – and if and how they can be controlled for the benefit of human health and wellbeing.

BBC Monitoring

The parish of Binfield Heath, 3 miles from Henley, includes Crowsley Park, 160 acres encompassing an eighteenth-century manor house, swathes of Forestry Commission land, and the nerve centre of BBC Monitoring – a sinister-sounding organisation whose headquarters are at Caversham Park near Reading. Its role is to receive, monitor, translate and report on worldwide mass media. It was founded in 1939 to report on foreign broadcasts and propaganda for the benefit of the War Cabinet. Whatever the world whispers, Crowsley Park hears it first.

It played a crucial role in the Second World War, and was the foremost ear to the ground during the Cold War, the collapse of Soviet and East European communism, the ensuing civil war in the former Yugoslavia, and the dramatic developments in North Africa and the Middle East during 2011.

Historically, BBC Monitoring has been funded by stakeholders such as the Cabinet Office, and subscriptions from the Ministry of Defence. But from 2013/14 funding will be via the BBC licence fee: that's £25 million that the BBC somehow has to siphon off from its income, at a time when the licence fee itself has been frozen at £145.50 until 2016. Hence ongoing threats and fears surrounding 'minority interest' services such as BBC 4. The World Service, threatened with the axe, was saved after intense protest, but the BBC now has to fund that service too (it was formerly paid for by the Foreign Office).

Crowsley's horse and cow-grazed parkland, concealing its forest of satellite dishes and radio antennae, has limited public access via two footpaths.

Westmill Wind Farm

Watchfield, near the border with Wiltshire, has the largest co-operative wind farm in the country, in operation since 2008. The 2,400 members of Westmill Wind Farm raised funds to construct five 49m-high wind turbines, each bearing three 31m-long blades, on the old airfield (now an organic farm). They are connected to an electricity sub-station on the site, generating pollution-free energy for 2,500 homes. The turbine towers have no detrimental effect on the crops being grown below; and if you want to see how we'll all manage to survive in the future, a peek at Watchfield is a good starting point.

Isis Innovation

The famously agricultural Oxfordshire has, paradoxically, the highest growth rate of high-tech jobs in the UK, most of them rooted to Oxford University. Technology transfer and consultancy company Isis Innovation, based in Summertown, Oxford, has spun out around seventy companies since 1997. It has a trading turnover of around £7.4 million and files an average of one patent application a week.

The other high-tech hot beds are Oxford's Begbroke Science Park and Magdalen College's Oxford Science Park, coalitions of University researchers and start-up companies.

8

UNIVERSITY, COLLEGE AND SCHOOL

Oxford University has no central campus or administrative area – the closest it has to a symbolic centre is the Sheldonian Theatre, where degrees are handed out each year. It's a forest masquerading as a tree, a self-satisfied maze of contradictory golden Cotswold stone that turns all prose purple.

The origins of the University are to be found in 1167, when King Henry II banned English students from studying at the University of Paris. Oxford had teaching establishments prior to this, but it was 1167 that kick-started the glorious chaos that today passes for a cohesive institution.

The syllabuses, goals and bad habits of friars and students who had been denied the delights of Paris scattered themselves across Oxford, the details coming before the concept that would unify them. The complex mess that resulted was reinterpreted as a stroke of genius and called a University. Independent halls, and later Colleges, came together in federation under the motto *Dominus illuminatio mea*, 'God is my light', as if only Divine illumination could make proper sense of it all.

Sheldonian Theatre.

The University, for all its impenetrable antique air, has never stood still. Bits have been added, bits have been removed: fourteenth-century Queen's College was rebuilt in the eighteenth century; many of the 'ancient' gargoyles and carvings of Magdalen, New College and Brasenose were installed in the twentieth century to replace wind- and rain-eroded predecessors; the forty-year-old giant heads surrounding the Sheldonian Theatre are the third lot to stand here since the building was erected in the 1660s; St John's, founded in 1555, has a quadrangle dating from 2010; while the latest College, Green Templeton, an amalgamation of two recent foundations in 2008, is centred on the eighteenth-century Radcliffe Observatory.

Oxford University doesn't make much sense – or, rather, it resists attempts at logical analysis – but it works. And its quirks, eccentrics, legends and treasures are endless. You could spend every holiday for the rest of your life visiting bits of the University, and still not run out of surprises.

THE COLLEGES IN CHRONOLOGICAL ORDER

University College (full name: the Master and Fellows of the College of the Great Hall of the University of Oxford, 'Univ' for short), High Street, founded 1249. Legend says King Alfred got there even earlier, founding it in AD 872.

Balliol College, Broad Street, founded 1263. Alumni's world-changing publications include John Wycliffe's English Bible (*c.* 1395), Adam Smith's *Wealth of Nations* (1776), and William Beveridge's society-shaking *Report* (1942).

Merton College, Merton Street, founded 1264. It has the world's oldest academic library, where books were originally chained to the shelves or kept in locked chests.

St Edmund Hall (aka Teddy Hall), Queen's Lane, founded 1278. The sole survivor of the original mediaeval academic halls, but officially a College since 1957.

Exeter College, Turl Street, founded 1314. Alumni include fantasy kings J.R.R. Tolkien and Philip Pullman.

Oriel College (has also been known as the College of St Mary, and King's College), Oriel Square, founded 1326. Named after one of the

View of High Street from St Mary's Church.

College's original properties, la Oriole, which had a large Gothic bay window, an 'oriel'.

The Queen's College (originally the Hall of the Queen's Scholars at Oxford), High Street, founded 1341. Knocked down and rebuilt in the eighteenth century, it is famous for its weekly lunchtime organ recitals and the Boar's Head Ceremony.

New College (full name: New College of St Mary), Holywell Street, founded 1379. The grounds contain a pristine section of the original town walls, and a large mound said to have been raised over a pit of plague victims.

Lincoln College (full name: the College of the Blessed Mary and All Saints, Lincoln, in the University of Oxford), Turl Street, founded 1427. Once a year, on Ascension Day (forty days after Easter Sunday), children gather in the Quad to scramble for hot coins while their elders drink ground ivy ale.

All Souls College (full name: College of All Souls of the Faithful Departed), High Street, founded 1438. A £654 loan to King Charles I in the 1640s was not repaid until 1857.

Magdalen College, High Street, founded 1458. A requiem Mass is sung here each year for the late lamented Henry VII.

Brasenose College (aka BNC, full name: the King's Hall and College of Brasenose), Radcliffe Square, founded 1509. Named after a nose-shaped 'brazen' (brass) door knocker smuggled to Stamford in the 1330s and returned 550 years later.

Corpus Christi, Merton Street, founded 1517. Graduates include James Oglethorpe, who went on to found the American State of Georgia in 1733.

Christ Church College, St Aldates, founded in 1524 as Cardinal College, refounded in 1536 by Henry VIII. It holds the record for producing prime ministers – thirteen so far.

Trinity College (full name: the College of the Holy and Undivided Trinity), Broad Street, founded 1554. Charles I took all the College silver during the Civil War, to make into coins to pay his army.

St John's College (full name: St John Baptist College), St Giles', founded 1555. The College's Kendrew Quadrangle is the University's most recent feature, opening in 2010.

Jesus College (full name: Jesus College in the University of Oxford of Queen Elizabeth's Foundation), Turl Street, founded 1571. It maintains strong links with its spiritual home in Wales.

Wadham College, Parks Road, founded 1610. Associated with gay rights, since a former warden fled the city in 1739 after homosexual allegations.

Pembroke College, St Aldates, founded 1624. Dr Samuel Johnson dropped out of the College in 1729 due to lack of funds.

Worcester College, Walton Street, founded 1714. Original mediaeval cottages on site only survived because the eighteenth-century demolition programme ran out of money.

Regent's Park College, Pusey Street, founded 1810 (moving from London's Regent's Park). Its oldest resident is a ninety-plus-year-old tortoise called Emmanuelle.

Keble College, Parks Road, founded 1870. Controversial when first unveiled, with its neo-Gothic 'polychromatic brickwork' design, it was nicknamed 'Holy Zebra' by detractors.

Bridge of Sighs.

Hertford College, Catte Street, founded 1874 as a merger of Hart Hall (1282) and Magdalen Hall (1448). It is famous for the Bridge of Sighs over New College Lane, linking two parts of the College.

St Stephen's Hall, Marston Street, founded 1876. A training ground for Anglican clergy and other theologians.

Wycliffe Hall, Banbury Road, founded 1877. Unashamedly evangelical Christian establishment, true to its founders.

Lady Margaret Hall, Norham Gardens, founded 1878. A revolutionary foundation, enabling women to study in Oxford for the first time.

St Anne's College, Woodstock Road, founded 1879 as the Society of Home Students. It was granted full College status in 1952. The original ethos was to allow women to study at Oxford without having to join one of the existing Colleges.

Somerville College, Woodstock Road, founded 1879. Once dubbed 'the blue-stocking college', amongst its many female high achievers were Indira Gandhi, Margaret Thatcher, Esther Rantzen and Iris Murdoch.

St Hugh's College, St Margaret's Road, founded 1886. Its youngest member was mathematical genius Ruth Lawrence, who joined in 1983 aged twelve.

Mansfield College, Mansfield Road, founded 1886. Originally established to enable religious dissenters to study at Oxford – an odd concept in today's pluralist, secular society.

Harris Manchester College, Mansfield Road, founded in Oxford in 1889, with College status in 1996. Originally located in Manchester, and enjoying stints in York and London before settling here.

St Hilda's College, Cowley Place, founded 1893. Established for women, the first male was not admitted until 2008.

Campion Hall, Brewer Street, founded in 1896 by Jesuits – and still highly religious. The present hall was designed in the 'Delhi Order' style by Sir Edwin Lutyens, prime architect of New Delhi.

St Benet's Hall, St Giles', founded 1897. Established so that monks from Ampleforth Abbey (North Yorshire) could take degrees at Oxford.

St Peter's College, New Inn Hall Street, founded 1929. It gained full College status in 1961. Received London evacuees from Westfield College in the Second World War.

Nuffield College, New Road, founded 1937. Founded by William Morris (Lord Nuffield) of Morris Motors fame.

St Antony's College, Woodstock Road, founded 1953. Established to attract international graduates for the study of international history, politics, philosophy and economics.

Linacre College, St Cross Road, founded 1962, with College status in 1986. Named after Thomas Linacre, one-time physician to Henry VIII, who founded the Royal College of Physicians.

St Catherine's College, Manor Road, founded 1962. Built on a water meadow which later became a rubbish tip, the accumulated rubbish raising the ground above flood level.

St Cross College, St Giles', founded 1965. Set up by the University to soak up the growing number of graduates unable to find room in the existing Colleges.

Wolfson College, Linton Road, founded 1965. Prides itself on being the most egalitarian and liberal of all the Oxford Colleges.

Kellogg College, Banbury Road, founded 1990, with College status in 1994. Established by the Kellogg Foundation, whose founder Will Keith Kellogg invented the cornflake.

Blackfriars Hall, St Giles', founded in 1994 by Blackfriars Priory, itself founded in 1221 and refounded in 1921. Students only study Philosophy and Theology, with a side order of English Literature, British History and Classics.

Green Templeton College, Woodstock Road, founded 2008. It was formed through a merger of Green College (est. 1979) and Templeton College (est. 1965), and is centred on the eighteenth-century Radcliffe Observatory, which was modelled on the Tower of the Winds in Athens.

FICTIONAL COLLEGES AND ALUMNI

There are at least sixty examples of Oxford College invention and re-naming in fictional works, including Thomas Hardy's *Jude the Obscure*, where Oxford is Christminster, Balliol is Biblioll, and the forbidding Rubric College and the deathly Sepulchre and Sarcophagus Colleges are less than subtle references to dusty old Academia.

Balliol became Baillie in the TV series *Yes, Minister*, while *Yes, Prime Minister* gave rise to Hacker College. Colin Dexter made several name-switches in the *Inspector Morse* novels, a tradition continued in the later TV dramatisations and the spin-off series *Lewis*.

'Foxe' is Corpus Christi in Philip Pullman's *His Dark Materials*, a reference to the College's seventeenth-century founder Richard Foxe. The same author replaces Wadham with Gabriel, Exeter with Jordan, and invents St Michael's and St Sophia's.

'Judas' was sourly coined by Max Beerbohm in *Zuleika Dobson* for Merton; Anthony Trollope invented Lazarus College in *Barchester Towers*; and Stephen Fry adopts St Mark's in *The Stars' Tennis Balls*, which had earlier been coined by Margaret Yorke in her Patrick Grant detective novels.

Evelyn Waugh came up with Scone College in *Decline and Fall*, and the name was perpetuated in the novels of Kyril Bonfiglioli, where

Scone College refers to Balliol. John de Balliol was a Scottish king who was crowned at Scone in 1292.

Shrewsbury College is the favoured ruse of Dorothy L. Sayers in her Oxford classic *Gaudy Night*, thought to be based on Somerville.

Mythical Oxford and its Colleges have spawned famous occupants too, of course. They include King Memphric, founder of the city; King Lud, first-century dragon hunter; Chaucer's Clerk of Oxenford; Captain Hook; Charles Ryder and Sebastian Flyte; Jay Gatsby; Lord Peter Wimsey; Bertie Wooster; James Bond; Sir Leigh '*Da Vinci Code*' Teabing; Lyra Silvertongue/Belacqua of Philip Pullman fame; Rupert Giles of *Buffy the Vampire Slayer*; and a couple of X-rated ones: Fox '*X Files*' Mulder, and Charles Xavier of the X-Men.

TEN STATISTICS ABOUT OXFORD UNIVERSITY TODAY

It is made up of thirty-eight Colleges and six halls, all self-governing.

There are approximately 13,000 undergraduates and 10,000 postgraduates (plus another 18,000 students at Oxford Brookes University).

Only 1.1 per cent of Oxford students drop out, compared with a national average of 8.6 per cent, and more than 90 per cent of graduates find jobs or further courses within six months.

Forty-two per cent of students are postgraduates, and, of these, 61 per cent come from outside the UK (compared to 15 per cent of undergraduates).

Forty per cent of academic staff are of non-UK origin.

The University has offices in New York, Tokyo and Hong Kong, plus 190 alumni groups in over seventy countries.

Oxford University Press (OUP) is a department of the University and the world's largest university press, with offices in more than fifty countries, and more than 5,000 employees worldwide.

Oxford University is a founder member of Oxfordshire Business First, a network of public and private sector partners; while the student society Oxford Entrepreneurs, with over 4,500 members, is the largest free business and entrepreneurship society in Europe.

Oxford has the largest university library system in the UK. Most of the 100-plus sites are managed by the Bodleian Libraries, which holds more than nine million printed items – its new Book Storage Facility in Swindon is large enough for eight million items on 153 miles of shelving.

The University's six museums and collections are visited by over two million people every year. The six are the Ashmolean (established 1683, the oldest museum in the UK); the Museum of the History of Science (housed in the Old Ashmolean, the oldest surviving purpose-built museum building in the world); the University Museum of Natural History; the Pitt Rivers Museum; the Bate Collection of Musical Instruments; and the Christ Church Picture Gallery.

FRIAR BACON

Friar Roger Bacon (1214–94) was the first pre-eminent University genius, an advocate of empirical methods in scientific study. Legend dubbed him a magician, working from his alchemist's laboratory on Folly Bridge. The laboratory was known as Friar Bacon's Study, or Bacon's Folly (hence the bridge's name), a bridge-straddling squat tower pulled down in 1779. But he was simply ahead of his time, a scientist and mathematician in an age of superstition. He was responsible for the oft quoted 'A little learning is a dangerous thing, but none at all is fatal'.

He was a practical joker too: when some scholars from Cambridge University visited the city, Bacon is said to have disguised himself as a thatcher. The Cambridge men were taken aback when he proved to be a great versifier – and seeing that lowly thatchers were so clever, they didn't dare stay to meet the actual scholars.

TOWN VERSUS GOWN

'Town versus Gown' riots – i.e. Oxford townsfolk versus University students – were not new in 1355; but that year was a watershed, with a conflict that kicked off on St Scholastica's Day, 10 February.

Town versus Gown riot.

In the Swindlestock Tavern at Carfax, a group of students and priests complained about the poor quality of the beer. The landlord, who was also Mayor, cursed them, provoking one of the students to throw a pot of beer at his head. That was it. Tables went over, fists escalated into broken bottles, and then into bows and arrows, knives and cudgels. St Martin's Church bell at Carfax summoned the 'Town', and the bell on the University's Church of St Mary summoned the 'Gown'.

The Mayor called in reinforcements from outside the city – about 2,000 – who advanced chanting, 'Slay, slay! Havoc, havoc! Smite fast! Give good knocks!' Some of the University's halls were ransacked and in total, over three days, sixty-two students were killed. The Mayor appealed to King Edward III to take the Town's side, but he opted for Gown.

The Mayor, his bailiffs and successors had to attend a Mass for the souls of their dead victims every St Scholastica's Day; and the top section of the church tower at Carfax was knocked down, to prevent the Town from using it as a surrogate castle, as they had in the past.

Even more drastically, the Town had to swear a resurrected oath (first formulated after similar Town/Gown troubles in 1213) recognising the University's privileges and pre-eminence in the city. They did this each year, and had to go on bended knee to the Vice-Chancellor of the University, with sixty-two symbolic citizens, and hand over sixty-two silver pennies as perpetual compensation. Meanwhile, the 'Town and Gown' division remained as bitter as ever just below the surface.

St Martin's Church.

Memory dies hard in Oxford, and this ritual humiliation and one-upmanship was only abolished in 1825. At the 600th anniversary of the St Scholastica's Day riot in 1955, hatchets were finally buried when the Vice-Chancellor gave an honorary degree to the Mayor of Oxford in the Sheldonian Theatre, and in turn was made a Freeman of the city at the Town Hall.

OXFORD'S OTHER PLACE

'Excellence in Diversity' is an apt motto for Oxford Brookes University, an amalgamation of Colleges and institutions that seems to have been infected by the higgledy-piggledy origins of neighbouring Oxford University. It began life as the Oxford College of Art on the ground floor of the Taylor Institution on St Giles', joined in 1891 by a School of Science with which it merged, in 1934, to become the uncatchily named 'Oxford City Technical School, incorporating the School of Art', with John Henry Brookes (1891–1975) as Vice-Principal. It spread out over nineteen buildings throughout Oxford, was renamed 'Oxford College of Technology', and moved into much needed new buildings at Headington in the 1950s and '60s.

The institution became Oxford Polytechnic in 1970 and is currently sprawled at various bases, from Wheatley in the east to the former Westminster College at Harcourt Hill in the west, with Headington, Headington Hill and Marston Road in the middle. Since 1992 it has borne the Oxford Brookes name, after its first Vice-Principal.

Clementine Ogilvy Spencer-Churchill, wife of Winston Churchill, was the titular inspiration for Lady Spencer College of Education, built at Holton in 1966. It merged with Oxford Polytechnic in 1974, and now forms the heart of Brookes' Wheatley campus.

Drastic rebuilding has recently taken place at the Headington site, off London Road and Gipsy Lane, all taken at a bit of a dash following the usual wrestling matches with local council and residents. At one point, demolition was taking place before the final go-ahead for the new build had been given.

A Blue Plaque to John Henry Brookes was unveiled at his former home at 195 The Slade, Headington, in 2011.

EDUCATION BEYOND OXFORD

Oxford & Cherwell Valley College has a name which appears to state very clearly its geographical location. But it, too, has a confusion of campuses, largely the result of it being a merger between Oxford College of Further Education, North Oxfordshire College in Banbury and Rycotewood College in Thame. The latter relocated to Oxford in 2005, at which point the 'Oxford & Cherwell Valley' tag was adopted, to reflect the opening of a new campus further up the Cherwell at Bicester. In 2010 it spread its wings further, taking over Reading College.

Wroxton College is a Jacobean manor built on the foundations of a former abbey, and currently serves as the overseas campus of an American university. The lease had been sold to Trinity College, *A yard at Wroxton.*

Oxford in 1932, and in 1965 it passed to New Jersey-based Fairleigh Dickinson University. Here, American students are promised an experience of the 'quintessential English village scene'.

Since 1946, Shrivenham has been fighting for pre-eminence. In that year, the **Royal Military College of Science** (RMCS) was established on the Beckett estate, part of the Defence Academy of the United Kingdom. It provides Higher Education not just for the British Armed Forces, but for the Civil Service and the Government, and their equivalent personnel from other countries too.

Tucked away in the stately 1611 Yarnton Manor, north of Oxford, is the **Oxford Centre for Hebrew and Jewish Studies** – part of the University but independent (a typical University paradox). It was founded as a charity in 1972 by Dr David Patterson, and is the foremost centre for Jewish studies in Europe.

Abingdon School celebrated its 400th anniversary in 1963. In 2006 it celebrated its 750th. You don't have to do the maths: this was the result of a change in tradition rather than a rift in time and space. The school used to trace its establishment to 1563, but this was always known to be a re-foundation date. The current hierarchy takes the earliest mention of the institution, in an Abingdon Abbey charter of 1256, as the starting point.

Meanwhile, historians believe the whole thing started even earlier, citing a document from 1100 that mentions 'Richard the Pedagogue' as a local school headmaster. The name was only bettered when 'Flogging Tom' Woods (1716–53) took up the reins – and used them violently, no doubt.

A new suburb, complete with school, is being unveiled on **College Fields** next to Bodicote and neighbouring Banbury. The development, like all such green field upheavals, was controversial. Anti-estate campaigners got over 20,000 signatures on their petition in 2010, but to no avail: the county's latest school – along with 1,000-plus houses, shops, a restaurant, a pub, a new church and lots of preserved and newly planted hedgerows and green bits – is set to open.

9

SPORT AND LEISURE

BLOOD SPORTS

Bull-baiting

Bull-baiting was a popular national sport prior to the early nineteenth century, and Oxfordshire was a keen player. Animals were tethered and baited with dogs at the Bull Ring in the middle of Oxford, near the busy crossroads of Carfax. Bulls were also baited at Headington and other neighbouring villages, nearby Wheatley being so keen on its bullish games that its bouts continued until the sport's final suppression in 1832 – the last surviving bull bait in England.

Badger-baiting

William Gladstone, recalling his time at Christ Church in the 1830s, claimed that the College's chief pastimes were rat-killing, cock-fighting, otter-hunting and badger-baiting. A vicar at Wheatley spent much ink and passion in the mid-nineteenth century deploring the latter sport and imploring his parishioners to desist.

View of Carfax.

Deer-hunting

Kings and aristocrats have hunted deer in Oxfordshire since history began. There were deer parks in various places, including Woodstock/Blenheim, Wychwood, Beckley, Cornbury and Shotover. In 1820, a stag was hounded all the way from Blenheim Park to Oxford. Once in the city, it raced to Brasenose College and sought sanctuary in the chapel, which was conducting a service at the time. Regardless of protestations, the hounds were sent up the aisle.

In earlier days, the students of Oxford were fond of deer poaching – not in their backyard at Magdalen, but in the Royal Deer Park at Beckley on the edge of Otmoor. In the fifteenth century, the University was warned that if its students didn't cease their predations, the institution would be stripped of royal privileges.

Venison was on the Whit Sunday menu in many Oxfordshire villages. At Ducklington, huntsmen gathered at midnight and blasted on hand-made 'peeling horns', spirals of green willow bark pinned with blackthorns and fitted with a reed to blow down. Several villages joined the chase. The first man on the scene of the kill was entitled to the head and antlers, and the deer was then skinned at a local inn. The skin was distributed in strips, and brought good luck, and marriage, to anyone who wore a piece in his cap. The festivities lasted all the week, with the deer finally cooked and served on Saturday. The horns were peeled for the last time in the 1840s.

Fox-hunting

Oxfordshire has several long-established fox hunts on its territory, including the Heythrop, the Bicester and the Old Berkshire, founded by John Ward in 1783. In the hamlet of Bainton, an obelisk was erected in 1812 in memory of one of the Berkshire Hunt's most beloved hounds, Lady. She was kennelled at nearby Bainton Manor Farm, a seventeenth-century manor house and spiritual home of the Hunt. The Old Berkshire still chases across lane and field in these (officially at least) post-fox-hunting times.

Otter chasing

Rousham House, which has been in the same family since the 1630s, contains many follies – including a grotto under a mock-bridge, flanked by stone swans, surmounted with a stone Venus, and with the inscription: 'In Front of this Stone lie the Remains of Ringwood an otter-hound of extraordinary Sagacity.' An accompanying four-stanza poem includes a warning to any otter – 'Tyrant of the Cherwell's flood' – to stay away.

Hare coursing

Ann Richards was the sole child of Compton Beauchamp House owner Edward Richards, and inherited the estate when he died in 1728. She was renowned for her beauty, and many men coveted both her good looks and her fortune. But Richards was not interested – 'an utter foe to wedlock's noose' in her own words – lavishing all her attentions instead on the sport of hare coursing at Ashdown Park. She wrote her own epitaph, published in *Goodlake's Stud Book*, 1828:

> Reader, if ever sport to thee was dear,
> Drop on Ann Richards' tomb a tear,
> Who, when alive, with piercing eye,
> Did many a timid hare descry ...
> All arts and science beside
> This hare-brained heroine did deride; ...
> At books she laughed, at Pope and Clarke,
> And all her joy was Ashdown Park.
> But Ann at last was spy'd by death
> Who coursed and ran her out of breath.

Pope and Clarke were the pre-eminent poets of the day.

HORSE SPORTS

Jeddah

Adderbury Village Institute opened in 1898, built with funds donated by Major Larnach of Adderbury House. Larnach was a horse man, and his favourite nag was Jeddah, trained in the village and entered in the Derby in 1898 at odds of 100-1. Not only did Jeddah confound bookmakers by winning the race, he also went on to win Ascot. The result was a good deal of fame, and a huge deal of cash. Larnach spent part of it on the Institute, which still functions as a thriving part of village life.

Baulking Green

Baulking, a tiny village near Faringdon in the south-west of the county, gave its name to Baulking Green, a gelding horse of the Old Berkshire Hunt. He was a Cheltenham Festival champion on four occasions, during a brief but illustrious career from 1961 to 1969. After his performance in '68, he was commended in the annual point-to-point bible *Hunter Chasers & Point-to-Pointers* as 'just about the most gallant animal that ever looked through a bridle'. Baulking even has his own biography, *Baulking Green, Champion Hunter Chaser*, written in 1971 by Ron Liddiard.

Best Mate
In 2005, at the age of ten, Best Mate, dubbed 'the nation's favourite racehorse', died suddenly, inspiring headlines and lyrical obituaries in the national press. He was a bay gelding trained at West Lockinge Farm near Wantage, winning the Cheltenham Gold Cup three times in succession, 2002–4, and fêted as one of the greatest steeplechasers.

On 1 November 2005, Best Mate had a heart attack during a race at Exeter. Out of twenty-two races he had won fourteen, come second in seven, and met his doom in the last. His ashes were buried beside the winning post at Cheltenham, and a bronze statue of the horse flares its nostrils proudly in West Lockinge.

Hurlingham Polo Association
In addition to hunting and racing, horses are also an essential ingredient of polo, aka 'hockey on horseback'. There are approximately 2,000 human participants in the UK. The Hurlingham Polo Association, which drew up the first set of polo rules in 1874, has been based at Little Coxwell near Faringdon since 2000. It is the creator and upholder of the official rules of a game first introduced to the British Empire in the 1850s, when tea planters observed a bout on the India-Burma border at Manipur. But in historical terms they were latecomers: the first match is reckoned to have been held in the Middle East around 600 BC.

Quintain
Blackthorn, near Bicester, had a quintain until the early eighteenth century. This was a tall pole with a horizontal swivelling pole perched on top. A target was attached to the rotating section; a man on horseback would then charge at the quintain with lance or sword. The targets ranged from shields and hoops to actual seated men. The word derives from the Latin *quintana*, a street in a Roman camp where martial practice took place. The sport survives as 'tilting at the ring', extant in equestrian and military sporting circles.

MUSCLE POWER

Prizefighting
Freeland near Eynsham was once the haunt of pugilists, the sports of prizefighting and wrestling being very popular. Broken jaws and knuckles abounded at their rendezvous, Roslyn – a house built in

1738 and formerly known as 'Wrostling [i.e. wrestling] House'. The same association can be seen in the village's Wroslyn Road.

The James Figg pub in Thame commemorates prizefighter (bare-knuckle boxer) James Figg. He was born in the town in 1684 and was famous for the battle cry: 'Here I am, Jemmy Figg from Thame! I will fight any man in England!' He was crowned Champion of England several times.

On 3 December 1810, prizefighting reached its heyday at Shenington Hollow on the Oxfordshire-Warwickshire border, with a World Title contest between Tom Cribb and Tom Molineaux, a former slave from Virginia. After thirty-five bloody rounds, Cribb floored his opponent.

The couple met again the following year in Rutlandshire, before a crowd of 15,000. Cribb won after eleven rounds, his face so swollen with the pummelling that he could barely open his eyes. He retired in 1812 at the age of thirty-one, becoming a coal merchant, a part-time boxing trainer, and finally a London publican. He is in the International Boxing Hall of Fame.

Molineaux had a less happy ending. He ran up huge debts, became an alcoholic, and died of liver failure, aged thirty-four.

Singlestick
Singlestick contests were staged on Blackthorn Hill until 1823. The singlestick was a mock-sword made of wood, 1 yard long, used originally to practise the various moves needed when wielding backsword or sabre. In its more robust form, singlesticks was a type of 'cudgels', in which opponents aimed to bludgeon each other.

Kart racing
Shenington Kart Racing Club was founded in 1959 – the oldest such club in the UK. It hosts a twenty-four-hour pedal car race at the end of June. This is an endurance test, with a maximum of six drivers pedalling all day at average speeds of around 18mph.

Tug-of-war
At Tiddington, the River Thame forms the boundary between Oxfordshire and Buckinghamshire, and county rivalries are settled at the annual tug-of-war between Tiddington and neighbouring Ickford in Bucks. The rope spans the river, with a 5-yard gap between the riverbank and the nearest contestant. The team that gets hauled into the water loses.

The tug-of-war was first staged in 1953, to mark in eccentric fashion the coronation of Queen Elizabeth II. There are separate male, female, youth and veteran bouts; and in accordance with rules set down by the Tug-of-War Federation of Great Britain and the Tug-of-War International Federation (the sport being an Olympic event until 1920), there are eight tuggers in each team. The umpire stands mid-river to oversee the contest. The tuggers must be fully clothed, and wear no spikes in their boots; and the losers must buy the winners twelve pint bottles of beer and pay for an inscription on the Cup. Ten per cent of the proceeds is set aside for the rope fund. It is, indeed, money for old rope.

Aunt Sally
Aunt Sally is an Oxfordshire speciality in which players throw batons at a wooden skittle 'doll'. It may be an echo of the ancient sport of cock-throwing, where competitors threw at a live bird. It is said to have been introduced to the county by Royalist soldiers when Charles I set up court in Oxford during the Civil War. There are several pub leagues, with the season running from May to September.

DIFFERENT WAYS TO MESS ABOUT ON THE RIVER

Poohsticks
Poohsticks, invented by A.A. Milne in *The House at Pooh Corner* (1928), has grown in popularity over the years, and since 1984 there has been an annual World Championships. It takes place on the 91m stretch of the Thames between Day's Lock and Little Wittenham Bridge near Dorchester-on-Thames. Around 1,500 visitors turn out for the contest, many from abroad. There is an individual event and a six-person team event.

The lock-keeper had noticed people spontaneously playing Poohsticks, and came up with the idea of putting out some sticks and a collection box in aid of the Royal National Lifeboat Institution (RNLI). The event grew from there. It takes place in March (unless the flow of the river is too heavy, as it was in 2001 and 2010, in which case the Championships are cancelled), and is organised by the Rotary Club. The youngest winner of the single event was a five year old in 1996, and the team event has been won by Japan, Australia and the Czech Republic in recent years.

Oxford-Cambridge Boat Race

The Oxford-Cambridge Boat Race takes place every April on the River Thames. First staged in 1829, it now attracts up to 250,000 spectators plus millions of TV viewers. After all these years it is a closely run thing, Cambridge maintaining a narrow lead of 80-76 in 2012. This was a unique year in race history, with a swimming protester causing a re-start; a broken Oxford oar when the crews clashed; an unconscious crew member, victim of exhaustion; and cancellation of the Awards Ceremony for the first time ever, in recognition of a less than celebratory bout.

The Oxford University Boat Club's Oxford boat house went up in flames in 1999, torching the event's archive. A purpose-built boat house was opened in 2004 at Wallingford, and these are some of the many facts and figures to rise from the ashes:

The heaviest Oxford oarsman was Christopher Heathcote in 1990, at 110.22kg (17st 5lb). The lightest was Alfred Higgins in 1882, a mere 60.1kg (9st 6.5lb). The lightest cox, Hart Massey, weighed in at 32.66kg (5st 2lb) at the 1939 race.

The youngest oarsman in recent decades was Matthew Smith, eighteen years and eight months in 2000. The oldest was 2008's Mike Wherley, an American Olympic athlete, at thirty-six.

The smallest winning margin was 30cm, achieved by Oxford in 2003.

The only dead-heat was in 1877, announced confusingly by the judge as 'a dead-heat to Oxford by five feet'.

Cambridge hold the fastest course time – a sixteen-minute, nineteen-second victory in 1998. They also hold the slowest record – twenty-six minutes, five seconds in 1860.

Boats have sunk six times in the event's history, most spectacularly in 1912 when both teams sank. In 1984, Cambridge sank on their way to the starting line after hitting a moored barge.

The first woman to participate was Sue Brown, Oxford cox in 1981.

Boat Race umpire Boris Rankov holds the record for the most races, having manned the oars six times.

It is said that each member of the team trains for two hours for every stroke in the race; and it takes an average 600 strokes to get to the finishing line.

Henley Regatta

The five-day Henley Regatta, established in 1839, is the oldest event of its kind, predating all organised rowing clubs and organisations. As such, it is allowed to have its own rule book. It was originally an event for amateur rowers, and anyone who had received prize or income of any kind, or worked professionally with boats in any capacity, was not allowed to enter. But to attract only the 'right sort', the rules also barred anyone 'who is or has been by trade or employment for wages a mechanic, artisan or labourer' – later extended to anyone 'engaged in any menial activity'.

In 1920, the soon-to-be American Olympic rowing champion John B. Kelly Senior was told he could not compete, as he had served an apprenticeship as a bricklayer. Henley also pointed out that Kelly belonged to a boat club, which had been outlawed after its members raised money to pay for their trip to the regatta in 1905. Money from fund-raising still counted as payment.

Revenge was eventually exacted by Kelly's son, John B. Kelly Junior, who won the coveted Diamond Sculls event in 1947. His daughter made an even bigger impression on the world: she was actress-turned-Princess of Monaco Grace Kelly.

Similar embarrassment occurred in 1936, when some Australians were barred due to being policemen. According to the long arm of the oar, this made them 'manual workers'. In the storm that followed, the references to labourers, menial activities, etc., were erased from the rule book. In 1998, the last references to 'amateurism' were removed.

The regatta consists of straight head-to-head races over a 1-mile, 550-yard (2,112m) stretch of the Thames in July. Since 1851 it has been called the Henley Royal Regatta, with initial patronage from Prince Albert.

Henley's position close to two county borders is underlined by the fact that racing teams are assigned to the 'Berks' or 'Bucks' side of the race course. The Royal is not the only regatta in town, either. The same course hosts Henley Women's Regatta, Henley Veterans' Regatta and Henley Town and Visitors' Regatta too.

Eights Week

Oxford has many watery events on the Thames and Cherwell, the main one being Eights Week, aka Summer Eights, a four-day regatta contest between the Colleges. It takes place over five days in May, with around 1,800 rowers taking part. A cannon blast gets things underway, and a waterborne bout of dodgems ensues. Boats try to 'bump' the vessel in front, simultaneously avoiding being bumped by the one behind. The aim of a crew is to win the title 'Head of the River'.

Bathing

Parson's Pleasure (originally Patten's Pleasure) in the University Parks at Oxford was the city's concession to naturism. Closed in the 1990s, for centuries this section of the River Cherwell had been the place where gentlemen of the University would get their kit off and take a dip. John Sparrow, warden of All Souls, once refused to cover himself when a gaggle of girls came sailing by, doing the watery pole-dance demanded by punting. In defence of his over-exposure, Sparrow proclaimed, 'I don't know about you, but most people recognise *me* by my face!'

The city's other official riverside bathing spots have all vanished too, including Dames Delight for women and children, further along the river. Tumbling Bay was another *al fresco* bathing spot, behind the Botley Road allotments. These days, the justifiably popular outdoor bathing pool at Hinksey does its bit to compensate for the loss – though bathing costumes are required.

CUSTOMS, FAIRS AND GATHERINGS

Boar's Head Ceremony

St Giles' Church in Horspath near Oxford has a seventeenth-century stained-glass depiction of John Copcot stuffing a book into the mouth of a wild boar. This illustrates the legend of fifteenth-century student Copcot of Queen's College and Horspath. Walking through Shotover Forest reading Aristotle, he was surprised by a boar. He used the only weapon available, the book, and thrust it down the boar's throat with the words *Graecum est* – it's all Greek to me. In other versions, it is the expiring pig that utters the immortal words.

Copcot took the beast's head back to Queen's College in Oxford, which marks the occasion every year near Christmas with the Boar's Head Ceremony. The centrepiece is a cooked boar's head (the traditional first course at mediaeval feasts), crowned and garlanded with laurel, mistletoe, rosemary and small heraldic banners.

'The Boar's Head Carol' is sung, the earliest versions of which date from the fifteenth century. The song was recorded as a not-very-hit single by Steeleye Span in 1978.

The garlanding ceremony

Charlton-on-Otmoor maintains the ancient tradition of garlanding the rood screen in St Mary's Church on May Day. The screen is an ornate wooden structure, complete with rood loft and rood cross, separating the chancel (the bit that contains the altar) from the nave (the bit where the congregation sit). This kind of thing was once common to all English churches, but under Henry VIII's son, Edward VI, there was a rood awakening and all such screens, lofts and crosses were ordered to be destroyed.

Somehow Charlton's survived, and is the finest example in the country. During the garlanding ceremony, a cross of foliage is carried around the village and placed over the rood screen – until 19 September (one of St Mary's many feast days), when the cross is replaced by a new one. The garlanded cross is made to look oddly female, its base billowing out like a dress, and its flowers sometimes suggesting buttons and feminine decorations. Indeed, it is sometimes referred to as 'the Lady'. This suggests that it has replaced an effigy of Mary rather than a cross, a feature of every church in the country prior to the Reformation (see any existing Catholic church for details).

Bampton's May bank holiday

Bampton Morris has roots that probably stretch much further back than its earliest mention in the 1790s. The morris men dance on the late May bank holiday weekend, which also hosts the 'Shirt Race'. Teams consisting of two people in fancy dress, and a decorated trolley, race around the village pubs. This is organised by the tongue-in-cheek SPAJERS, or Society for the Preservation of Ancient Junketing.

Bampton Pumpkin Club

Bampton May Garlands are constructed on the May bank holiday Monday too, made from flower-decorated hoops fixed together to form a ball. But the most celebrated round vegetable item here is the pumpkin. The Bampton Pumpkin Club was formed in 1969 to celebrate enormous vegetables, and a competition takes place each October in which size is all important. Anyone with a fruiting body less than 20 kilos should not bother entering. The pumpkins, along with other vegetables, fruit and flowers are auctioned in aid of the elderly residents of the village.

Folk songs

The county has plenty of morris sides, including Headington Quarry. Folk song collector Cecil Sharp encountered the latter on Boxing Day 1899, subsequently making their concertina player, brick-maker William Kimber, one of folk music's first celebrities. Sharp's interest in Kimber's tunes inspired him to search for more musical treasures, kick-starting the English folk song revival. A Blue Plaque commemorating Kimber was unveiled in 2011, on the house he built on St Anne's Road, Headington. His grave, with concertina motif, is in Headington Quarry churchyard, close to that of C.S. Lewis.

Dancing

May Day and Whitsun (at the end of the month, a moveable feast replaced by the modern late spring bank holiday) were times for dancing. Not just morris teams, but anyone with the joy of spring in their heel. Matthew Arnold's 'Scholar Gipsy' mentions:

> Maidens, who from the distant hamlets come
> To dance around the Fyfield elm in May.

This celebrated tree is at Fyfield near Abingdon.

Healing wells

People from Finstock, Leafield, Milton, Shipton and Ascott (the latter three suffixed '-under-Wychwood') and other villages in and around Wychwood Forest used to gather water from supposedly curative wells on Palm Sunday. The most popular was the Wort Well in the heart of the forest, but Finstock folk favoured Lady Well at Wilcote. The water was mixed with liquorice, peppermint and sugar to make a sweet concoction, and was referred to as Spanish Water – 'Spanish Sunday' or 'Spanish Liquor Day' being secular names for Palm Sunday.

The Church never approved of the tradition, largely because it resulted in empty churches. The custom was actually banned in AD 963, but managed to survive into the 1960s, and is still kept alive by the likes of Wychwood Brewery, who allude to the custom in their literature. The section of forest with the old well is private, but opens every Palm Sunday for perambulations.

Wychwood Forest's name echoes 'Hwicce', the Saxon tribe who occupied this part of the island, and is also linked to the wych elm tree. The area is maintained through Oxfordshire County Council's organisation the Wychwood Project, which carries out conservation and woodland management work, involving as much of the local community as possible.

May Day hymns

1 May 1509 marked the completion of the bell tower of Magdalen College, one of Oxford's great landmarks. Since that date, Magdalen choristers have sung a hymn from the top of the tower every May Day morning, the original one being a requiem for King Henry VII, who had died on 21 April 1509.

Thousands gather in Oxford each May Day morning to hear the amplified choristers at 6 a.m.; to watch the morris men, Jack-in-the-Greens and street musicians; and to see if the Cherwell bridge-divers have evaded the police this year. The 'sport' is discouraged, the water being far too shallow for a drunken high dive, and there are frequent concussions and soggy newspaper reports.

Dragon and giant

Burford used to parade effigies of a dragon and a giant through the town at Whitsun and on St John the Baptist's Day (24 June). According to sixteenth-century historian Camden, this was a folk memory of an eighth-century battle fought nearby between the kingdoms of Wessex and Mercia.

Harvest cross-dressing

The odd custom of harvest cross-dressing died out in the first half of the nineteenth century. Ducklington, near Witney, was one of its strongholds. On the last night of the wheat harvest, the villagers provided women's clothes and ribbons for two young men, who dressed as women and sat with their two male partners as the horses brought home the last sheaves. The party was treated to cakes and ale.

Kirtlington Lamb Ale

The Kirtlington Lamb Ale took place on the three days after Trinity Sunday. During the festival a man carried the first-born healthy lamb of the season around his shoulders, its legs tied together with ribbons. At the end of the merrymaking, lamb pies were eaten. Chief among these was the Head Pie, containing the head and wool of one of the beasts. The standard pies were free, but the head pie was sold for a shilling.

In 1679, T. Blount gave a now discredited account of the Lamb Ale at Kidlington (a typo for 'Kirtlington'). He described how, when the lamb was released, 'the Maids of the Town having their thumbs ty'd behind them, run after it, and she that with her mouth takes and holds the Lamb, is declared Lady of the Lamb, which, being dress'd with the skin hanging on, is carried on a long Pole before the Lady and her Companions'. On the following day, the lamb was cooked by being 'part bak'd, boyl'd and rost'.

The Kirtlington pie-fest ceased in 1858, but the spirit of the event was revived in 1979. Kirtlington Morris got together and reinvented the Lamb Ale as a morris dance festival, with obligatory sheep-roast, taking place around the old Whitsun festival at the end of May or early June.

St Giles' Fair

Oxford's September St Giles' Fair in 1883 was reported as being the biggest yet, and less rowdy than in previous years. It had been a long-standing tradition for youths to assault evening promenaders at the fair with devices sold by stallholders for that purpose. This was dubbed 'the fun of the fair'.

Fire-crackers had been the original weapon, causing the occasional lady's hat to catch fire. 'Scratchers', rubbed on a victim and making a loud rasping noise, had been the next big hit, followed by water-pistols. But in 1876, such 'squirts, scratch-my-backs, and other instruments of personal annoyance' had been outlawed, and anyone caught selling them would forfeit their pitch at the fair.

Rubber whips made a brief appearance in the aftermath, along with flour, bran, sawdust and pepper to throw in promenaders' faces; but, by 1883, the official assault weapon had been emasculated: the local paper reported that 'amusement was limited by the Magistrates to the brushing of each other's faces by bunches of feathers or grass'.

1883 was marred, however, by the fair's first death. Frederick Burnard, a coachman, tried to light his pipe in mid-ride on the steam roundabout. He lost his balance, fell and fractured his skull. The owner of the ride was cleared of blame afterwards – the coroner noted that steam rides were inherently dangerous, but that this was the first such death he had heard of in thirty years.

The thing that nearly sank the fair was not the danger element, but the incidence of youths running up to ladies and kissing them. In 1888, and again in 1893, the immoral effects of such 'rowdyism and swagger' were debated, and a ban was proposed. But somehow the event survived.

St Giles' Fair is one of the largest and widest street funfairs in Europe, on account of the odd dimensions of St Giles'. Meanwhile, Abingdon's Mop Fair at the beginning of October claims to be the longest and narrowest such event, stretching half a mile through the centre of town and all the way down Ock Street.

Electing the Mock Mayor

In 1885, Thomas Hemming of Abingdon, the Mayor of Ock Street, resigned after twenty-five years in power. The title passed to his son, William, who inherited a rare survival of the once widespread 'Mock Mayor' office. The Mock Mayor's job was to voice the will of the common people, in the days before they had any means of formal representation, and to deflate the official Mayor.

The Mayor of Ock Street still exists in the twenty-first century, but candidates should be warned that the Mayor's power is limited: the only intervention he is allowed to make in the everyday running of local life is 'to turn an old sow out of the gutter and take her place himself', according to the rule book.

The title is the preserve of the Abingdon Traditional Morris. Their version of the story says that in 1700, an Abingdonian named Morris organised an ox-roast and distributed the food to the poor. The feast was so good that fights broke out to claim the ox's horns. Opposing sides formed on either side of the Ock Street-Vineyard divide. On 21 June 1700, the Ock Street faction claimed victory.

Since then, the morris men have carried these horns in their midst, mounted on a wooden, garlanded ox-head effigy. The fight is commemorated each year on the Saturday nearest to 19 June with dancing, a small fair, and the election of the Mayor of Ock Street, official keeper of the horns. All residents of Ock Street (site of the Morland Brewery from 1711–1999) can vote, and the Mock Mayor acts as Squire of Abingdon Traditional Morris for a year.

Competition is still hot for the post: in the 2010/11 election, the three candidates notched up sixty-five, sixty-one and fifty votes respectively. The Mayor's sword of office is said to have been carved from a cudgel used in the original brawl.

Woodstock also installs a Mock Mayor annually, with an accompanying family-friendly village fête. As part of the ceremony, the entire Mock Corporation is dunked in the River Glyme. Banbury and Headington formerly had Mock Mayor events too.

House at Market Place, Banbury.

Bun throwing

Whenever there is an occasion of local or national celebration, buns are launched from the roof of Abingdon County Hall Museum. Recent events meriting rolls on the drum include the Queen's Golden Jubilee in 2002, the 450th anniversary of the town's Royal Charter in 2006 and the Royal Wedding in 2011. The origins and significance of this have been lost, but a collection of varnished buns, some of them 200 years old, can be seen in the museum.

Grass-strewing

Shenington still observes the ancient custom of 'grass-strewing' for three weeks beginning on Whit Sunday. The floor of the church is covered with bundles of grasses, in a custom which originated from the need to replace the pestilential floor coverings in churches at least once a year.

Beating the Bounds

Each May, the parish of St Michael at Northgate in Oxford Beats the Bounds. This parish boundary perambulation has survived in spite of physical obstacles. In fact, it is the obstacles that make it so much fun, and which lure sightseers from across the world.

Armed with willow wands, the bounds-beaters walk a traditional circuit, thrashing each boundary stone and shouting, 'Mark! Mark! Mark!' This seems particularly appropriate at the boundary which sits behind glass in Marks & Spencer on Queen Street, marking the juncture of three parishes. There are halts in two other shops, a pub and the Town Hall. A section of old city wall is scaled, the University cathedral is beaten, and the final flagellation is in the grounds of Oriel College. Heated pennies are then thrown from the roof of Lincoln College down into the Quad, for the children to scramble over while the grown-ups sip ground ivy beer. In the old days it was the accompanying choirboys who were beaten, not the stones, to encourage them to remember the boundaries.

Hobby Horse Festival

On the first weekend in July, Banbury hosts the Hobby Horse Festival. It is the largest gathering of these colourful folkloric beasts in the world, ranging from horse-head-on-a-stick creations to ancient traditional characters such as the Minehead Hobby Horse, resembling a small ship rather than an equine. The horses have always been associated with dance and song, and there is plenty of that to be enjoyed. The event includes Cock Horse Racing, in honour of the 'fine lady on a white horse' who was spied by the cock-horse riders at Banbury Cross in the nursery rhyme.

10

FOOD AND DRINK

Various towns and villages are associated with foodstuffs, particularly Banbury and Oxford. Witney used to be known for 'the four Bs': bread, beer, beauty and blankets; and a local rhyme mentions 'Woodstock for bacon, Bladon for beef'.

Fertility Cake

Bampton Morris has an ancient Fertility Cake tradition. The delicacy sits in a cake tin, impaled on the ribbon-decorated blade of the team's sword-bearer. Pieces of the cake are handed out while the dancers caper, and those who receive a slice are expected to make a donation to the 'Squire's Treasury'. The cake brings good luck, and recipients used to store a piece over the following twelve months.

Organic

North Aston is spiritual home to the modern organic ethos. Local producer North Aston Farms was one of the first in the country to adopt wholly organic farming methods for meat and milk. The village is also home to North Aston Organics, vegetable producers who provide the certified stuff via farmers' markets, fairs and a veg box delivery scheme throughout the county. In addition to these earth-friendly credentials, North Aston plays host to the environmentally conscious Nicholson's plant and tree nursery.

Celebrity chefs

Oxfordshire has many celebrity chef connections. Sophie Grigson lives in Cumnor: she is the daughter of Jane Grigson, whose collection of books and cookery notes is kept by Oxford Brookes University. The institution also keeps the National Brewing archive, and the collections of chef Ken Hom and the late drinks expert Michael Jackson.

Jamie Oliver has an extremely popular restaurant on George Street in Oxford; Antony Worrall Thompson runs the Greyhound gastropub in south Rothersfield; and Raymond Blanc's restaurant and hotel, Le Manoir aux Quat' Saisons, is in the old manor house at Great

Milton. He also has branches of his Maison Blanc Boulangerie and Pâtisserie in Oxford, Burford and Henley.

BANBURY

The **Banbury Cattle Market** is no more. Its 17 acres in Grimsbury are occupied by housing, the market having closed in 1969. It had been in operation for over 800 years, moving to the Grimsbury site from out of town in the 1920s. At its height it was the biggest meat market in Western Europe, with beasts driven here from as far away as Scotland.

The town still holds a 'biggest' title in the food world, however – Ruscote-based **Kraft Foods, Banbury** being Europe's largest coffee processor. This is the latest in a long line of food- and animal-related trades in the town, which was once synonymous with cakes, cheese, ale and wool.

Banbury cakes are oval pastries filled with currants, similar to Eccles cakes. Sometimes called Banbury buns, they date back to at least 1586, when baker Edward Welchman first sold them at his shop on Parsons Street. However, there are other recipes claiming to date back to the thirteenth century, and legend maintains that they were brought back by Crusaders from the Holy Land. 'Real' cakes are made to a secret recipe, of course, but the basics are currants, candied peel, nutmeg, brown sugar and a dash of rum.

Banbury cheese was originally a strong, hard cheese made in flat rounds. These odd dimensions made them synonymous with thinness. In *The Merry Wives of Windsor* (1597), Bardolph retorts with 'You Banbury Cheese!' when Slender calls him a 'coney-catching rascal'. John Marston's play *Jack Drum's Entertainment* (1601) uses the same insult: 'Put off your cloathes and you are like a Banbury cheese, nothing but paring.'

OXFORD

Markets
In 1776, a local guidebook claimed that **Oxford Covered Market** was 'universally allowed to exceed everything of its kind in the kingdom'. John Betjeman concurred in the 1950s, claiming that its Georgian air somehow made anything bought there seem better than stuff from other shops.

The edifice today is largely the work of Thomas Wyatt the Younger in 1890. The site itself was chosen after the 1771 Mileways Act outlawed street trading in St Aldates which, as Fish Street, had been the main market area of Oxford. But even this second version has not remained entirely safe from redevelopers. A lobby in the 1940s pressed for a Covered Market Mark III, complaining of the 'gloomy and congested' atmosphere and claiming that 'the carrying of bloody carcasses across crowded pavements does not increase their pleasantness'.

The bloody carcases have, so far, survived (if you will forgive the paradox). Headless deer, pigs strung up by their heels, and gently rotting game – not to mention sluggish crabs and lobsters, claws tied like contrite pickpockets – are still part of the market's visceral attractions. It also offers Oxford Blue, Oxford Isis and College White – cheeses produced by the Oxford Cheese Company.

Oxford Marmalade
Deciding to sell jars of his wife's marmalade from his shop at 84 High Street in 1874 was Frank Cooper's master stroke. As soon as Oxford dons and students acquired the taste for it, lured by the 'Oxford Marmalade' tag, its fame was sealed. In those days, Oxford supplied most of the high-ranking jobs in the Empire, and Frank Cooper's marmalade went with them.

Cooper's opened a purpose-built factory in 1900 on the corner of Hollybush Row and Park End Street; but, in 1967, the company was acquired by Premier Foods, moving production out of Oxford and leaving its former premises, the Jam Factory (currently an arts and theatre venue) unpreserved.

Jars of Frank Cooper's accompanied Scott to the Antarctic, and real and imaginary fans include the Queen and James Bond.

Oxford livestock
Oxfordshire has an eponymous chicken, the **Oxford Brown**, and also its own sheep, the **Oxford Down**. The latter has a distinctive dark skin with a heavy white fleece, forming a woolly fringe above the eyes. It is the largest and heaviest of the British 'Down' breeds, developed in the 1830s after crossing Cotswold, Hampshire Down and Southdown sheep. The centre of breeding was the former wool-capital of the county, Witney.

Oxford lamb, sometimes called Oxford John, is a dish of seasoned lamb or mutton, sliced thinly, formerly popular at the Oxford Colleges.

Oxfordshire has its very own breed of pig, the **Oxford Sandy & Black**, which has a dedicated society and website. The breed – also known as 'Oxford Forest Pig' and 'Plum Pudding' – reached its present form more than 200 years ago. After a low point in the 1940s, when just one or two boars were licensed each year, the animal now has a firm foothold in several rare breed collections.

Oxford sausages, sometimes featuring this beast, have no fixed recipe, but tend to include sage and lemon. **Pig brawn** is another county speciality; but those who dream of milkmaids must look elsewhere. A travellers' guidebook of 1860 noted: 'One may look in vain for a milkmaid throughout the county, as that office is always allotted to men or boys. Brawn is made in great quantities on the large farms.'

FRUIT AND VEG

Apricots
In the Middle Ages, the Lord of the Manor at Aynho, on the Northamptonshire border, used to demand part of his tenants' rent in apricots. The combination of good limestone soil and the warm stone walls enabled the trees to flourish. Some of the sunnier cottages of Aynho still have apricot trees climbing their walls.

A similar plan came to fruition at Glympton near Woodstock in the nineteenth century. The fruit from the village's twenty-odd apricot trees was sold to cover the 30s rent. And if money can be said to grow on trees here, it also flourishes underground. When the almshouses were built in 1949 by the owner of Glympton Park, a hoard of Stuart coins was found, probably deposited here during the 1640s, when both Royalist and Parliamentarian troops used the village facilities.

Oranges
Beatrix Havergal was a great fan of oranges, particularly those grown on the Seville orange tree at the Orange Tree House in Waterperry. The fruit inspired her to establish the Waterperry School of Horticulture, a ladies' residential college, in 1932. It closed its doors when Havergal retired in 1973; but the spirit of the place very much lives on in its current guise as Waterperry Gardens, with a garden centre, nursery, extensive gardens, Saxon-founded church, shops, Museum of Rural Life and the National Collection of Saxifrages. The orangery itself was restored to its original Victorian splendour in 2010.

Easter Bunny

In 2010, during the annual Waterperry Easter Bunny Hunt, children stumbled upon a dead baby rabbit, laid out prominently on a border in the Mary Rose Garden. The cry of 'Easter Bunny's dead!' cast a shadow over the spring afternoon.

Watercress

Watercress used to be grown in industrial quantities at Cassington, the village's name coming from Old English *Caersentun*, meaning 'cress growing town'. It used to be a difficult crop to clean: if not done sufficiently, it can carry waterborne bacteria that cause stomach upsets.

In modern Oxfordshire the surviving watercress haven is at Ewelme, which has a 6.5-acre nature reserve based on watercress beds that were planted (probably from existing cress sources) in the 1890s. Commercial growing came to an end in 1988, but since then the Chiltern Society has purchased the site. It raises money for the beds' upkeep via Friends of Ewelme Watercress Beds fundraiser nights, and by charging visitors £2 a head.

Volunteers do much of the heavy work, clearing the beds of invasive species such as reed and mace, which crowd out the timid cress. In June 2010, the volunteers included two parties of fifteen airmen from nearby RAF Benson. Ash clouds from an erupting Icelandic volcano had grounded them, and they were twiddling their thumbs until someone suggested they use these, and all their other fingers, in helping to clear the overgrown watercress beds.

Ironically, the cress from Ewelme cannot be sold. Modern health and safety requirements would involve analysing the ostensibly clean water once a month, at £50-plus each time. Instead, the former delicacy is composted.

Swede

The swede made a wholesale invasion of the fields of Oxfordshire in the early years of the nineteenth century. Quickly dropping its earlier names of rutabaga and cabbage-rooted-turnip, the early days were not without their problems. Good seed was hard to come by, and one farmer complained in 1805 that the crop he had raised from poor seed was like 'cabbage stalks without the cabbage'. Even sheep were said to turn up their noses at some of these early varieties.

Bach Flower Remedies

In the 1930s, proto-homeopath Edward Bach of Brightwell-cum-Sotwell established his theory of Bach Flower Remedies. The reasoning behind these minute dilutions is that dew collecting on flower petals, and subject to early morning sunlight, acquires the plant's inherent healing properties via osmosis, properties present in such infinitesimally small amounts that they cannot be detected as such.

Bach added the sunlit dew to a solution of brandy and an equal measure of water to create a 'mother tincture', diluted as appropriate. When the amount of dew was insufficient, Bach suspended flowers in spring water, treated them to the early morning sun's rays, and got the same results. Vendors still claim that the dilutions contain the 'energetic' or 'vibrational' properties of the flower and its particular healing trait.

Bach remedies are not homeopathic in the strict sense of the word, as they do not involve carrying out repeated dilutions known to homeopathists as 'succession'. But what really separates Bach Flower Remedies from others is that they contain no plant parts, just dew. And the original choice of each plant for each condition was decided not by the study of active ingredients or existing herblore, but by Bach's self-professed psychic connection to the plants themselves.

The Bach Centre in Brightwell-cum-Sotwell still produces its founder's thirty-eight flower remedies; although these days mass production is carried out by Nelsons of Wimbledon, to feed an ever-growing international demand.

LIQUID REFRESHMENT

Coffee

Coffee was first sold in Oxfordshire in 1650, by a man called Jacob in St Peter-in-the-East parish, Oxford. It was said to have been imbibed by those 'who delight in novelty' and, according to seventeenth-century Oxford historian Anthony Wood, 'others who esteemed themselves either Virtuosi or Wits'. Today's army of on-the-hoof coffee drinkers are the descendants of these early fashion victims.

Nathanael Konopios of Crete was the man who actually introduced the beverage to the city, though. He was living at Balliol College, having been sent by Greek Orthodox Church Patriarch Cyril Loukaris in the 1630s, in an attempt to find common ground with Protestant nations. The religious mission was a failure, but coffee worship has never left the city. Its oldest surviving outlet is Queen's Lane Coffee House, founded in 1654.

Port
In May 1762, George III's cellars were stocked with bottles of port. This was the first time that the fortified wine had seen the inside of a royal cellar, but its impact was almost immediate. A month later, port had drawn level with perennial favourite, Bordeaux claret, as the wine most commonly glugged by the royal household.

Blenheim Palace's George Spencer, 4th Duke of Marlborough, Lord Chamberlain of the Royal Household in 1762, was responsible for port's invasion of the royal tastebuds. He was a great fan himself, and between January 1763 and December 1767, an impressive 20,022 bottles of booze were delivered to his three stately piles, almost half of the total going to Blenheim, and half of it consisting of port.

By the 1780s, Marlborough and the royals were not alone: port was a resident favourite in the household of any self-respecting aristocrat or fashion-following, gouty socialite in England.

Old Speckled Hen
Abingdon used to produce MG cars for British Leyland. One particular vehicle, used as the factory's runaround motor, was nicknamed the Old Speckled 'Un due to its battered, spattered state. The name, with a small tweak, was adopted in 1979 by Abingdon brewer Morland for its now famous ale Old Speckled Hen, brewed to commemorate MG's fiftieth year. However, Morland has since left town too, Greene King of Bury St Edmunds buying the name and relocating production to Suffolk.

Breweries
Morrells of Oxford has also closed its doors, but some breweries are still in production. These include old-timers Brakspear at Witney (formerly based at Henley), who also produce Wychwood beers; Appleford Brewery from Brightwell-cum-Sotwell; Loose Cannon of Abingdon; the Shotover Brewing Company in Horspath; the White Horse Brewery at Stanford-in-the-Vale; and several other micro-breweries, including Compass in Oxford.

Hook Norton has one of the country's last working Victorian tower breweries. It has cherished its alcoholic industry ever since Vikings tried to steal all the beer during a raid in AD 913 (well, I'm sure they would have done, given half a chance). The brewery, which doubles as a brewing museum, opened in 1849. Before 2006 it was all powered by a Buxton & Thornley 1899 steam engine, and this still drives the mashing equipment, mill and sack hoist. As a further link to bygones, horse-drawn drays still deliver barrels to the village pubs.

Ale verse

Tipples have waxed and waned in popular taste. Oxford College records are full of site-specific brews, including spiced Pope Wine, Cider Bishop (featuring jellied calves' feet), Grace Cup, Wassail Cup, Oxford Punch, Swig and Brasenose Ale. The latter, called a 'matchless beer', inspired the lines:

Shall all our singing now be o'er since Christmas carols fail?
No! Let us shout one stanza more in praise of Brazenose Ale! [*sic*]

This is just a snippet from a long history of 'ale verses' penned at the College, dating back to at least 1700. New verses were recited each year by the College Butler on Shrove Tuesday, to accompany the latest brew of in-house beer. The College brewhouse was demolished in 1889, but the much-missed ale verse tradition was rehydrated in 1909, even though the beer was, and is, now brewed elsewhere.

The Temperance Movement

The Temperance Movement was allied to the non-conformist church, and sought to remedy the problems of alcohol-related ill-health and abuse. This was not the simple prudery of abstemious spoil-sports: alcoholic children were common in many cities, and the neglect and violence associated with hard-drinking parents was the stuff of nightmare newspaper stories.

In 1832, the Oxford Board of Health printed a warning in the local newspaper, underlining the link between cholera and drunkenness:

But especially beware of drunkenness, for *it has been found to bite as a serpent and to sting as an adder*. Many who have raised their cup in merriment to their lips, have in agony lamented their excesses, and at their deaths have left a last legacy of warning to the drunkard. Let all beware who think no cost too great for the purchase of present pleasure – Death smites with its surest and swiftest arrows the licentious and intemperate – the rash, fool-hardy, and imprudent.

The teetotallers adopted a zero-tolerance approach, and their publications included reports from county agents whose task was to stamp out the demon drink. George Best, the official Oxfordshire agent, gave a typically upbeat report in the March 1845 edition of the *National Temperance Chronicle*:

> I have succeeded in introducing the principles of teetotalism into four villages, noted for vice, drunkenness, and profanation of the Sabbath.

Bayworth and the Baskervilles

A case in point could have been Bayworth Manor House. Built in the seventeenth century, it didn't survive more than 100 years. Its owners, the Baskervilles, fell into decay due to booze and dissolute living, and dragged the house down with them. Excavations on the site by a local secondary school discovered a stash of wine bottles from the Crown tavern in Abingdon, and it was cheekily speculated that they had stumbled upon the weapon with which the House of Baskerville was levelled.

11

NATURAL HISTORY

ROCKS AND FOSSILS

The Launton meteorite

Several billion years ago, when the earth was a body of newly compressed matter spinning dizzily around the sun, the story of Launton in Oxfordshire began. Much of the material of the solar system was destined for an endless orbit in the Asteroid Belt, a kind of rock dumping ground between Mars and Saturn; but one such iron and nickel-stuffed lump broke free of its brothers and sisters, and eventually picked up the gravitational field that sent it hurtling down to its rendezvous with Launton in 1830.

The *Magazine of Natural History* published an account of the descent, describing:

> ... the fall of a meteoric rock on Monday, the 15th day of February, 1830, at half-past seven in the evening, in the garden of John Bucknell ... at Launton, near Bicester, Oxon. Its descent was accompanied with a most brilliant light, which was visible for many miles around, and attended with a triple explosion, which was described to me, by a person who heard it at the distance of four miles, as resembling the rapid discharge of three ordinary guns. It penetrated some newly dug mould nearly a foot deep ... A man named Thomas Marriot was passing near the garden at the moment, and states that it came rapidly towards him from the north-east, not perpendicularly but obliquely, appearing about the size of a cricket-ball; and that expecting it would strike him, he instinctively lowered his head to avoid it.

The Launton meteorite, of the variety known as 'ordinary chondrite', can be seen in London's Natural History Museum – the one in Oxford's Museum of Natural History is a replica.

Geology

When proto-geologist and engineer William Smith hit rock bottom, a new science was born. In recognising that the earth's underlying rocks, and their accompanying fossils, had been laid down in a predictable sequence – the Principle of Faunal Succession – he unearthed a new science: geology. The Principle was of great practical and economic significance to the burgeoning coal industry, for which Smith did much of his early work. His geological map of 1815 (developed from an initial sketch made in 1801) was the first of its kind in the world, and is astonishingly accurate.

Not that it did Smith much good. His lowly origins precluded him from aristocratic scientific circles, and his work was ruthlessly plagiarised. At his low point he was committed to debtors' prison, and his genius was only officially recognised when the Geological Society of London honoured him with their highest medal in 1831, and called him the Father of Geology. Luckily, Smith survived a further eight years – long enough to enjoy the knowledge that in a world of small steps and small minds, he had made leaps of truly geological proportions.

Two notable and diverse locations are named after him – a museum in Scarborough, and a crater on Mars.

Fossils

Oxfordshire is rich in fossils, and was an important source of material for early scientists trying to work out the implications of petrified shells and bones. In the north-west of the county, Jurassic limestone, shale and sand form the Cotswold hills – the origin of the famously golden-yellow Cotswold stone that decorates many a town and village in these parts. Locally tagged seams include Banbury marble, Stonesfield slate and Forest marble (named after Wychwood Forest). These have yielded a rich fossil harvest, including extremely rare prehistoric mammal remains.

There are further Jurassic seams in the region of Oxford: more limestone, and clays including the eponymous Oxford clay. The Cretaceous makes its dramatic contribution with chalk downlands, the most famous outcrops being the Uffington White Horse and its hill. The valleys around here were carved by rivers during the last Ice Age, when earth and rock were frozen, allowing water to run over the usually porous chalk. Cretaceous clays and greensand crop up too. All of this indicates a submarine past: largely shallow seas and coastal lagoons, a typical geological irony in a region as far from the present-day sea as it is possible to be in England.

Fossils caused headaches for scientists such as seventeenth-century Robert Plot, first keeper of the Ashmolean Museum in Oxford. Fossilised seashells found inland posed the obvious question: how did they come to be here in the rocks of Oxfordshire, so far from the sea?

One popular theory was based on the Biblical story of the Deluge, of Noah's Ark fame. But Plot ruled this out for various reasons: if the Flood had been a gentle accumulation of water, it would not have evicted the shellfish from their sea beds and left them stranded on hills and mountains; and, if violent, would have scattered the animals rather than leaving them in the neat, ordered beds that the fossil grounds presented. He noted that many crowded fossil shellfish beds suggested established colonies that would have needed longer than the Flood's forty days to become rooted. He also refused to believe that England could experience earthquakes sufficient to raise cockle beds to hilltop level.

Plot had a couple of alternative theories, however. He suggested that urinous salts – i.e. fossilised puddles of urine – may have been involved in some deposits. But his chief theory was that fossils were formed at the beginning of Creation, when God was 'dispersing the Seminal Virtue of Animals through the Universe'. When this divine outpouring hit water, it resulted in living shellfish; but if the creative juices hit 'an improper Matrix' such as earth, they produced shellfish-shaped, inanimate stones.

Belemnites

The various quarries and gravel pits of Oxfordshire have yielded thousands of belemnites over the years. They are the calcified remains of long-extinct squid-like creatures – although the familiar bullet-like 'belemnite' is just the tail end of an internal structure, a bit like the 'bone' inside a modern cuttlefish, so beloved of pet budgerigars. They are often found in great abundance in one spot, and such sites are known as Belemnite Battlefields, echoing the folkloric belief that the shells are bullets or spear-tips. More commonly, they were thought to be solidified lightning bolts, a notion preserved in their name, which comes from the Greek root *belem*, meaning a dart. Robert Plot asserts that they were used to cure various medical conditions, from dispersing kidney stones, curing oral ailments and drying open wounds, to treating eye diseases in horses. Powdered belemnite was still being blown into horses' eyes for this purpose in early twentieth-century Oxfordshire.

Dinosaurs

Dinosaur remains were even more baffling than shellfish. The cast of a **Mosasaurus** skull in the Oxford University Museum of Natural History (OUMNH) was taken from a specimen unearthed at Maastricht in the 1770s. It caused a genuine sensation in a society with no concept of extinct ancient animals. The cast was given by pre-eminent natural historian Georges Cuvier to Oxford University's William Buckland in 1818.

The grand matriarch of dinosaurs, however, is **Megalosaurus** ('huge lizard'), a carnivore from the Middle Jurassic. Robert Plot of the Ashmolean mused on a fossilised thigh bone, discovered at Cornwell near Oxford in the seventeenth century, rejecting the theory that it must belong to a huge elephant introduced into the country by the Romans. Sticking his neck out, he suggested it was evidence of an ancient race of humanoid giants. Only in the early 1800s was this thigh bone assigned to Megalosaurus, after the aforementioned William Buckland discovered further remains at Stonesfield. He described them after receiving advice and input from Georges Cuvier, and named the animal *Megalosaurus bucklandii*. In 1842, Richard Owen, professor of the Royal College of Surgeons in London, placed Megalosaurus in a new class of animals – the dinosaurs.

Buckland was to have an impressive portfolio of locally unearthed prehistoric animals named after him. In addition to *Megalosaurus bucklandii*, he has the flying reptile *Rhamphorhynchus bucklandii* and the Jurassic mammal *Phascolotherium bucklandii* – 'Buckland's Pouch-beast', also known as the Stonesfield Mammal, after the village quarry where it was found.

Cetiosaurus oxoniensis, translating as 'Oxford whale lizard', was a 'brontosaurus'-type dinosaur. The first specimen appeared at Chipping Norton in 1825. The remnants on display in the OUMNH were discovered in 1860 by watchmaker Mr Chapman – after they had been shovelled to one side by oblivious workmen at a quarry near Kidlington.

In 1879, dinosaur bones were uncovered by workmen at the brick pit on Cumnor Hurst, south-west of Oxford. A man whose name, sadly, has not been recorded, salvaged the bones, and they later landed on the desks of George Rolleston, Linacre Professor of Anatomy and Physiology at Oxford University and Joseph Prestwich, Professor of Geology. The bones were ascribed in 1880 to a new species, *Camptosaurus prestwichii*, 'Prestwich's flexible lizard', a member of the Iguanodon family.

The Jurassic **Eustreptospondylus oxoniensis**, 'Oxford well-turned vertebra', belonged to the family that spawned the more celebrated Tyrannosaurus rex. The OUMNH's specimen is the most complete carnosaur ever discovered in Europe. It was discovered in 1871 in a Summertown brick pit, the same pit from which many of the museum's own bricks were sourced: the physical remains of Eustreptospondylus' world enfold you as you explore the edifice.

The earliest known stegosaurs were unearthed in Oxfordshire clays. The remains are very bitty, and several earlier finds have since been re-classified as other species. Most embarrassingly on the re-identification front, some 1887 dorsal plates – the bony structures that project along the length of the **Stegosaurus**' back, its signature feature – turned out to be the armour of a large, bony fish.

Ardley is the only place in Britain to have been given the status of Site of Special Scientific Interest (SSSI) on account of its fossils – or, more accurately, its ichnites. In plainer words: dinosaur footprints. The 165 million-year-old tracks embedded in the limestone, discovered in 1997, were made by a **Megalosaurus** and a herd of **Cetiosaurus**, wandering the Jurassic shoreline.

The SSSI designation came in 2010, the Megalosaurus tracks having been installed at Woodstock's Oxfordshire Museum in 2009. There are also casts of the Ardley tracks on the front lawn of the OUMNH. (And, proving that Ardley's natural history glory days are not all in the past, there is a colony of rare great crested newts within the SSSI.)

The installation at the museum in Woodstock was not without its hitches. When the Dinosaur Garden – consisting of plants that flourished during the beasts' Jurassic heyday – opened with a fanfare, a few eyebrows were raised at the rather lurid, crudely jointed, day-glo replica Megalosaurus at the heart of it all.

Staff had worked through the night to get the garden ready ... but the big model dinosaur planned for the middle simply wasn't ready. Instead, the life-size model upon which the finished sculpture was based was dusted down and hastily erected.

The proper beast is now in place, of course. And anyone who says, 'I preferred that bright orange and yellow one you had before,' is escorted from the premises.

THE OXFORD DODO

The dodo (*Raphus cucullatus*) has been described as 'the most extinct of all extinct animals'. It has come to symbolise the very concept of extinction, a status reinforced by its adoption as the logo of the Durrell Wildlife Trust, the conservation organisation founded in Jersey by the late, great naturalist, author, *bon viveur* and champion of captive breeding, Gerald Durrell. But apart from Jersey and the bird's native island, Mauritius, it is Oxford which will be forever associated with the dodo.

This is on account of the specimen in the Ashmolean Museum, and the dodo in *Alice's Adventures in Wonderland*, which was inspired by the museum's artefacts. There were, however, even earlier Oxford dodos at the University's Anatomy School at Christ Church. At the time of the Restoration (1660), its collection included two specimens.

Tragically, the Ashmolean's dodo – originally described as 'Dodar from the island Mauritius; it is not able to flie being so big' – was in such a sorry state by 1755 that the body was burnt, with just the head and feet preserved. The ravages of time, the carnivorous efforts of dermestid beetles, and the relatively primitive nature of contemporary taxidermy, were all to blame.

Hilaire Belloc, in his *Cautionary Verses* (1907), commemorated the Oxford dodo:

> The voice which used to squawk and squeak
> Is now for ever dumb –
> Yet you may see his bones and beak
> All in the Mu-se-um.

It is sobering to learn that this Oxford dodo represents the most complete remains of a single specimen, being the only bones to retain any soft tissue. You may be disappointed to learn that the actual bits on display in the museum are casts, the original parts safely tucked away in store.

OTHER NON-NATIVE SPECIES

Giraffe
In the 1850s there was an Anatomy Museum at Christ Church College, presided over by Henry Acland. As space was limited in the

Anatomy School, preparation of museum exhibits was carried out in an adjoining stable. This proved highly offensive to the coachmen and servants, who had to endure the terrible odours of macerated, boiling animals. One particular giraffe proved to be a maceration too far: the coachmen lodged an official complaint, and before Acland could respond, College servants evicted the offending beast, shovelling it into the middle of the road in St Aldates.

The carcass proved irresistible to one lucky dog, which grabbed the giraffe's tail and bolted. Observant visitors to the University Museum of Natural History will notice that parts of the giraffe exhibit's tail are a different colour to the other bones: they are, in fact, made of lead – replacements for the bits stolen by that opportunistic hound.

Turtle

Turtle shells decorate the kitchen walls at Christ Church College. One of these creatures arrived in 1834, en route to the soup course for a banquet in honour of the Duke of Wellington. William Buckland, lecturer, let his son Frank ride on its back in the College's ornamental pond. Frank then helped to cut off the turtle's head in the kitchens, noting that it bit a little boy's finger after the decapitation.

Alice Liddell was taken by Lewis Carroll to see edible Christ Church turtles too. She cried at the starving reptiles' soup-bound fate, and this was the origin of the sad 'mock turtle' in *Alice's Adventures in Wonderland*.

Christ Church hall interior.

The Tolsey, Burford.

Oxford Down sheep

Oxford Down sheep are encountered widely in the county, naturally enough. Sheep used to be the primary concern of Burford, which was for many centuries a centre for the British wool trade. The striking Tolsey building on the High Street, with its pillars and steeply-pitched M-shaped roofs, was the meeting place of wealthy wool merchants, and is currently a local heritage museum.

Bozedown alpacas

In the fields either side of Hardwick Road, in Whitchurch-on-Thames, are some other woolly beasts, the Bozedown alpacas. This is allegedly the largest breeding and stud centre for the animal in the country. Other pockets of alpacas can be found at Kennington, South Newington, Ewelme, Marston St Lawrence, Great Milton, Little Tew, Horton-cum-Studley and elsewhere. Farm animals can also be encountered at Farmer Gow's Activity Farm in Fernham and Millet's Farm and Garden Centre, complete with woolly pigs and wildfowl lake, at Frilford.

American signal crayfish

Other aliens are not so welcome: the red-clawed American signal crayfish (*Pacifastacus leniusculus*) was introduced in the 1970s by the Ministry of Agriculture, Fisheries & Food (long since re-jigged into other governmental bodies). It was released in supposedly enclosed areas of water, but soon escaped and now inhabits much of the Thames, Cherwell and neighbouring canals. The Americans drive out the native white-clawed crayfish and infect them with the fungal 'crayfish plague', undermine riverbanks with their deep burrows, and generally bring imbalance to the ecosystem.

Scientists hope that pheromone-soaked crayfish traps will help. They are placed on riverbeds, the theory being that sex-hungry foreign crustaceans will flock thither. The theory is unproven as yet, but alternatives have been slow in arriving – it is illegal to interfere with any crayfish, and they cannot be moved, caught for consumption, or used as bait without a licence. The law is obtuse: if one is netted by mistake, you are not allowed to throw it back, and nor can you eat it. A dilemma indeed.

Red kite
A happier invasion has been that of the red kite. This once common bird of prey had been extinct in England for a couple of centuries, but Spanish-bred birds released in the Chilterns in the 1990s have since multiplied and spread across much of Oxfordshire. It is now one of the county's signature birds, a wonderful local speciality.

Big Cats
All counties have their 'ABC' phenomena – Alien Big Cats. These are usually panther-like felines prowling in secluded spots, and always eluding both capture and camera – unforgivable in this age of mobile devices and instant pix. Oxfordshire's hotspot is around Banbury, thus falling comfortably into 'Beast of Banbury!'-type headlines. The occasional escaped exotic pet might be at the bottom of the scare, but that does not prevent the usual rash of cryptozoological theories about native big cats and/or ghostly manifestations.

Royal Menagerie and Monster Temple of Zoology
Exotic animal shows were a staple of the various fairs and sideshows that visited the towns of Oxfordshire in the nineteenth century. One of the leading exhibitors was William Manders, with his 'Royal Menagerie and Monster Temple of Zoology'. In 1859, he trumpeted the appearance of the country's first ever 'Chimpanzee or Black Eurang Outang', his contribution to the ongoing Darwinian-fired ape debate.

Some of Manders' other primates were not so well received. *Jackson's Oxford Journal* reported: 'On 10 September 1862 one of the monkeys fresh from a show at St Giles' Fair in Oxford attacked its keeper at a show in Thame, biting him so badly on the face and body that he was reported as being confined to bed.'

But Manders was a latecomer. William the Conqueror had established the county's earliest menagerie at Woodstock in the 1070s. Succeeding monarchs added to this royal zoo, which was eventually relocated to the Tower of London during King John's reign. The Oxfordshire collection included camels, owls and porcupines, and also had trickier exhibits such as lynxes, leopards and lions. These were not purely decorative: the free-ranging carnivores encouraged trespassers to keep out.

Cotswold Wildlife Park

The county's latest incarnation of the menagerie, the Cotswold Wildlife Park at Burford, takes a more welcoming approach to the peasantry, who pay for entry to this beautifully maintained conservation-focused collection with their cash rather than their lives. It opened in 1970 in the former grounds of the 1804 Bradwell Grove Manor, 2 miles from the town centre. Burford is also the headquarters of the Blue Cross animal welfare charity, founded in London in 1897 as Our Dumb Friends League.

Oxford Zoo

Between 1931 and 1937, the king of the jungle was Oxford Zoo, at Gosford Hill Farm, Kidlington (where the Thames Valley Police headquarters now stands). In the menagerie's last year – perhaps precipitating its closure – three wolves escaped. Two were shot dead soon after, but the third managed to evade the bullets for several days, allegedly killing thirteen sheep at a farm near North Oxford Golf Club, before being cornered in Summertown by a photographer from the *Oxford Mail*. According to the report, the intrepid employee commandeered a bike from a cyclist on the A40 and tracked the beast by following the sound of people shouting 'There's the wolf, there's the wolf!' He got his shot from 30 yards, and not just with his camera, sadly.

THE COUNTRYSIDE

Oxfordshire is the only county in England with three Areas of Outstanding Natural Beauty – the North Wessex Downs, the Cotswolds and the Chilterns. Beyond these tourist hot-spots, the county is largely agricultural. The most extensive ancient woodland is the Royal Forest of Wychwood, consisting of 530 hectares between the Windrush and Evenlode valleys. Wytham Woods near Oxford, owned by the University, covers 426 hectares. There are numerous other patches of forest, but in total Oxfordshire is less than 7 per cent woodland, compared with the national county average of approximately 8 per cent.

Port Meadow

The most ancient landscape in the county is the 120-hectare Port
Meadow on the north-east edge of Oxford, an unenclosed common
prone to flooding. It is said to have been given to the Freemen of
Oxford for their part in fighting off the Danish army in the late
ninth century. Grazing rights are still claimed on the meadow, and on
Wolvercote Common to the north.

In the seventeenth and eighteenth centuries, the tranquillity on Port
Meadow was occasionally broken by organised horse racing; and
during the First World War, it was a military airfield and Royal
Artillery base. In 1940 the war connection was continued, with a
camp set up to receive battered personnel evacuated from Dunkirk.

Farmoor Common

Farmoor Common was another wilderness, relatively untampered
with and pleasingly ancient, when, in 1967, a colossal amount of
concrete arrived, followed by lots of water. The ancient landscape had
been transformed into Farmoor Reservoir. Its primary purpose is to
water the distant town of Swindon in Wiltshire.

Ostensibly a haven for birdwatchers, you are not allowed near the
water itself unless you are a member of the sailing clubs based here.

'I like the ways these old brick garden walls run unevenly down
to Letcombe Brook,' wrote Poet Laureate John Betjeman in the
1972 poem 'On Leaving Wantage'. It was the beginning of a close
association between the poet and the stream, which runs prettily
through the village of Grove: the Letcombe Brook Charitable
Trust was established as a memorial to Betjeman, and Letcombe
Valley Nature Reserve opened in 2010. It lies near Letcombe Regis,
and consists of 19 acres centred on the stream. Specialities include
water voles, kingfishers, lampreys, crayfish, five species of bat, and
traditionally pollarded willows.

FLORA

Poplars

When a row of poplar trees was cut down at Binsey near Oxford, poet
Gerard Manley Hopkins was outraged. 'Felled, felled, are all felled
... Ten or twelve, only ten or twelve strokes of havoc,' he fumed in
'Binsey Poplars (Felled 1879)'. He was particularly angry to find that
they had been used in the construction of the Great Western Railway.

The poet's hot air is deflated somewhat by the fact that poplars seldom live more than 150 years, and the ones in question were past their peak – as indeed are the ones that were planted to replace them. Some have blown down, and some are due for the chop, to be replaced by new saplings. This is as it should be. Only humans value museums: permanence in nature is an illusion conjured by our own mortality.

Celebrity trees

The county has other celebrity trees, including the oak tree near Chilswell, used as a muse by Matthew 'Dreaming Spires' Arnold; the Poem Tree on Wittenham Clumps; the steel-supported twisted cherry tree by St Mary's Church on Oxford's High Street; the seven giant sequoias planted in the University Parks in 1888; and J.R.R. Tolkien's favourite tree, an Austrian pine (*Pinus nigra*) in the city's Botanical Gardens.

OneOak Project

In January 2010, a 222-year-old oak on the Blenheim Estate was cut down as part of the OneOak Project. It was the object of close study, of 'tree art', carpentry, and even of a new recipe. Oxfordshire-based chef Raymond Blanc honoured the tree's memory by utilising its sawdust (byproduct of a Toot Baldon furniture-maker) and creating a new dish, OneOak Salmon, its chief ingredient smoked on the wood shavings.

The oak is thought to have seeded naturally from an acorn. As part of the project, children planted 250 acorns on the site.

Oxford ragwort

Some smaller members of the plant family are closely linked with the county. In the 1790s, a hardy Sicilian species of ragwort, *Senecio squalidus*, escaped from the Oxford University Botanical Gardens and found itself at home. Oxford ragwort was amongst us. The old crumbling walls of Oxford reminded it of its dusty homeland in Sicilian lava fields by Mount Etna, and it never looked back, in spite of efforts to contain it. It has since colonised opportunistically in railway sidings, wasteland and cracks in pavements, and can now be found across most of the British Isles. Like the other members of the Senecio family it is poisonous, causing irreversible liver damage if ingested.

Ivy-leaved toadflax

Oxford weed, Oxford plant or Oxford ivy – aka ivy-leaved toadflax (*Cymbalaria muralis*) – is a native of mainland Italy that followed

Oxford ragwort's example, colonising stone walls and wasteland, first across Oxford, and then the rest of England.

Holton Park oak tree

Holton Park was a late Georgian mansion, built in the early nineteenth century to replace Holton's old manor house. In 1948, after a stint as a US-run war hospital, Oxfordshire Education Committee converted it into a grammar school for girls, and it is currently Wheatley Park School for eleven to eighteen year olds. Its oldest inhabitant is an oak tree: with a circumference of 9.7m, this beauty has been growing slowly since its first mention, in the Domesday Book of 1086.

Plant Heritage National Collection

The Plant Heritage National Collection consists of nationwide locations specialising in the main breeding stock of various flowers – the gold bullion of the floral world. Oxfordshire holdings include the Kabschia and Engleria saxifrages at Waterperry Gardens – tiny, hardy plants beloved of rock gardens; three types of aster are kept at Upton House near Banbury; brunnera, with their heart-shaped leaves, and blue-flowered omphalodes are nurtured at Gallowstree Common; the blue-flowered ceratostigma and yellow-flowered lysimachia are kept at Wolfson College in Oxford; clematis climb anything they can at Shillingford's aptly named Clematis Corner; succulent evergreen euphorbias are doted on at Oxford's Botanical Gardens; and tropical, leafy alocasias can be found at Newington Nurseries near Stadhampton.

FAUNA

Great tits

Ironically for a relatively forest-poor county, the wildlife and ecology of Wytham Woods has been studied for longer than any other comparable area of woodland in the world. For example, everything we know about the great tit was observed here.

Badgers

Another creature closely scrutinised at Wytham is the badger. In spite of 50 per cent of all the wood's badgers being slaughtered on roads, there are still an approximate 200 active individuals at any given time, making this a veritable badger city, probably the largest concentration in the world.

Swifts

In addition to the Chiltern red kites and Wytham Woods' great tits, the county's other most celebrated bird is the swift – specifically, those which make their home in the tower at Oxford's University Museum of Natural History. Studies here have shown that, on average, swifts live for six years, but can manage up to eighteen. In foul weather the chicks can go without food for ten days, withstanding 50 per cent weight loss. They also have to endure the attentions of parasitic louseflies, *Crataerina pallida*, which live exclusively in and around swifts' nests, sucking approximately 5mg of blood from their museum victims every day.

Observations in and around the tower's ventilation shafts – up to 147 pairs reside here, and approximately 100 new birds are ringed each year – have been ongoing since 1948, when David Lack, head of the Edward Grey Institute at the Department of Zoology, established the Oxford Swift Research Project. It is one of the longest continuous studies of a single bird species in the world. There is a dedicated book on the subject, *Swifts in a Tower*, the first edition of which appeared in 1956. These days we can all join in, via the Swift Webcam.

Bats

Horspath Tunnel, an old railway cutting at the village of Horspath, is a council-owned bat hibernaculum. It is an important roosting site for several species of bat, including Daubenton's. The ends of the tunnel have been sealed, with just small access holes; and a group of volunteers and experts has made the interior as bat-friendly as possible.

Similar things are afoot at the 382m Swerford Park Tunnel (aka Hook Norton Tunnel) near Swerford. Opened in 1881, the tunnel was closed seventy years later and sealed, to prevent human access and to allow bats to roost in peace.

Deer

Deer are the county's speciality, with large numbers of muntjac, roe and sika deer roaming free, and iconic herds of fallow deer at Magdalen College in Oxford. All four roam the 6,500 acres of Cornbury Park, and feed a thriving venison trade.

The Magdalen herd has been resident at the College's deer park – the Grove – for 300 years or so. They are culled to control numbers (usually in December, to the benefit of the butchers of Oxford's Covered Market), and are eaten on special College occasions. During

July and August the animals are relocated to Magdalen's Meadow to crop the grass – after local speciality, the snake's head fritillary, has set its seed.

Formerly the herd was limited to forty, this being the number of scholars according to the College's constitution. In 1939, the deer nearly found a new master when the Ministry of Food became responsible for all meat production in the UK. Somehow, the Magdalen dons managed to argue that their beasts were not meat, but, owing to their vital grass-cropping role, were part of the vegetation cycle of the Grove, and so evaded the Ministry.

Deer numbers are kept in check by marksmen from inside the College, to prevent the animals associating humans with gunfire and death. All of which used to come as a shock to students living on the ground floor of New Buildings – a favourite shooting spot – to which the deer stray very close. But since 1993, following a Junior Common Room petition, the deer are no longer culled in term time.

The Magdalen fallow deer begin their rut in October. College records still shudder at the gory events of 1993, in which the dominant stag, beaten by a one-horned challenger, was left in such a sorry state that he had to be shot. But the victor's glory was short-lived. In pursuing an elusive doe later in the rut, his foot and neck became entangled in a fence at the back of New Buildings. A new challenger took advantage and impaled the trapped stag, which broke its neck in its death throes.

Magdalen's deer have gone AWOL down the High Street on just one occasion in the last fifty years. Gone are the days when undergraduates would hunt them with bow and arrow as a rite of passage, or rustle them from the Grove (and into a celibate don's bedroom on one noteworthy occasion). T.E. Lawrence – of *Seven Pillars of Wisdom* and 'of Arabia' fame – once herded them over to All Souls College, to bring a little life to what he deemed a rather austere community. Sadly, this popular tale may well be apocryphal.

12

OXFORDSHIRE AT WAR

ROMANS, BRITONS, SAXONS, VIKINGS

Ælia Castra

Julius Caesar crossed the Thames near Wallingford, en route to a battle against the Britons at Cirencester in 54 BC; but it was not until AD 43 that the Romans actually conquered Britain. One of the settlements they established was Alchester, or Ælia Castra, 2 miles south of Bicester and located at an important crossroads. Stuffed with heavily armed soldiers, the site was abandoned after Rome withdrew from this far-flung corner of the Empire. One former resident, Lucius, was immortalised on a tombstone, salvaged for wall-foundation material by the thrifty Saxons. The inscription, as far as can be made out, reads (in translation):

> To the souls of the departed: Lucius Valerius Geminus, the son of Lucius, of the Pollia voting tribe, from Forum Germanorum, veteran of the Second Augustan Legion, aged 50, lies here. His heir had this set up in accordance with his will.

Lucius had settled far from home, Forum Germanorum being in north-west Italy.

Battle of Mons Badonicus

Badbury Hill, in the parish of Great Coxwell near Faringdon, is the site of the Iron Age fort known as Badbury Camp. It is thought by many to have been the 'Mons Badonicus', or Mount Badon, at which the indigenous Britons, abandoned by the Romans, defeated the invading Saxons some time between AD 490 and 520.

By the time the battle was being re-imagined in the ninth century by the historian Nennius, King Arthur was put at the centre of the action. Badon was the last in a long series of closely contested battles:

The twelfth battle was on Mount Badon in which there fell in one day 960 men from one charge by Arthur, and no one struck them down except Arthur himself, and in all the wars he emerged as victor.

This is the first mention of Arthur as a historical character, and the springboard from which a thousand legends were launched.

Cwichelm and Cynegils

In AD 613, the last local Saxon-versus-Briton battle took place near Bampton, where warlords Cwichelm and Cynegils boasted of slaying more than 2,000 Britons.

Battle of Burford

With the Britons banished, the English tribes continued the island's long tradition of civil war. In AD 752, the West Saxons rose up against their overlords, the Mercians, at the Battle of Burford. After a long and bloody conflict, Wessex's Cuthred defeated his Mercian foe Aethelbald and took the latter's golden dragon banner as a trophy. The victory was celebrated for many centuries afterwards: writing in the late sixteenth century, William Camden noted that Burford men parade a golden dragon and the effigy of a giant every Midsummer's Eve.

The battle took place on land still known as Battle Edge, beside Sheep Street. A stone sarcophagus, found on the site and presumed to belong to a leading participant in the conflict, can be seen near the West Gate of Burford churchyard.

Battle of Bensington

Benson was probably the site of the Battle of Bensington in AD 779, when Wessex King Cynewulf was defeated by Offa of Mercia, who gained Berkshire for his troubles.

Village of Ashbury

The village of Ashbury is first mentioned in AD 840, in a deed by which King Aethelwulf of Wessex handed it over to his minister, Duda. But the area must have been settled many centuries before then, as evidenced by the presence of the burial mound Wayland's Smithy, just 1 mile east of the village. This wonderful relic of a lost world was constructed between 3700 and 3400 BC.

There is a hillfort in the parish too, Alfred's Castle, constructed in the sixth century BC. It was named on the misunderstanding that it was constructed by ninth-century Wantage-born Alfred the Great, as a base during the wars against the Vikings, notably the Battle of Ashdown on 8 January AD 871...

Battle of Ashdown
...The Danish army under King Bagsecg, fresh from victory against the Saxons at Reading, marched to Ashdown to meet Wessex King Ethelred and his brother Alfred's armies. The Danes had the advantage of arms and tactics, but the Saxons had potentially more men – as long as they could summon them.

According to legend, the young prince rode to Blowing Stone Hill at Kingston Lisle and put his lips to the Blowing Stone. Only a skilled player could get a note out of this unpromising sarsen stone instrument, and only a man born to be king could make that note heard across the surrounding downs as far as White Horse Hill (a belief that still holds, if anyone fancies having a go).

Alfred hit the right note, and his troops came racing to his side. This seems a very precarious way of organising an army; but in his defence, Alfred used these early experiences to later organise his lands into an efficient army-raising machine, one of the achievements that was to give him the title 'the Great'. The crown fell to him in March 871, after Ethelred was killed in battle.

The Battle of Ashdown was a victory for Alfred, and King Bagsecg and his chief earls were killed. Legend says the former was buried in Wayland's Smithy. But there were heavy losses on both sides, and Viking victories were to follow. The wars only ceased when Alfred beat Danish King Guthrum to a standstill at the Battle of Ethandun (Wiltshire, 878), paving the way for the treaty that created the Danelaw, leaving Alfred's English with the southern rump of the island.

The Blowing Stone sits at the foot of Blowing Stone Hill in a private garden, looking like a fossilised Swiss cheese. Kingstanding Hill near Moulsford is also associated with the Ashdown campaign – it was where Alfred encamped and, presumably, stood.

St Brice's Day Massacre
John de Cella (*c.* 1152–1214) was born in Wallingford as John Hyde, son of the Lord of the Manor of Denchworth in Berkshire. He is widely known as John of Wallingford, and was Prior of Holy Trinity Priory in Wallingford and later Abbot of St Albans. He is far more

renowned as a historian, poet and physicist. His most celebrated work is *Chronica Joannis Wallingford*, a historical chronicle covering the period 449 to 1036.

One of the events he captures is the St Brice's Day Massacre of 13 November 1002, in which irate Saxons (under instruction from King Ethelred the Unready) slaughtered all the Danes they could find.

The massacres were carried out in various places in the English-held rump of the island, including Oxford. The violence provoked the invasion, in the following year, of Danish and Norwegian King Sweyn Forkbeard, who was subsequently installed as King of England in 1013. His son Cnut inherited the crown in 1014.

John de Cella gives an interesting root cause for the unbridled hatred that sanctioned the St Brice's Day bloodshed, and ironically ushered in this Danish dominance. He wrote:

> The Danes, thanks to their habit of combing their hair every day, of bathing every Saturday and regularly changing their clothes, were able to undermine the virtue of married women and even seduce the daughters of nobles to be their mistresses.

The massacre in Oxford took place at St Frideswide's Church (now Christ Church Cathedral), where the city's Danes had taken refuge. The Saxon contingent set fire to the edifice and slaughtered the survivors. The event was the stuff of unsubstantiated legend until 2010, when a mass grave at St John's College was unearthed, containing what are believed to be the bones of thirty-odd violently terminated Vikings.

King Canute

Legend equates Cherbury with the Dane Cnut (King Canute), who became ruler of England in the eleventh century. Cherbury was an important stepping stone to that achievement, according to the story. Cnut and his men were unaware that the Saxons from nearby Uffington Castle hillfort were making the 6-mile trek to Cherbury, armed to the teeth, in an attempt to eradicate the Danes. An enterprising shepherd boy saw the Saxons approaching, though, and warned Cnut. He rallied his army and marched out to meet the foe. The two armies fought at the crossroads between Charney Bassett and Buckland, and Cnut was victorious. The site was afterwards named Gainfield.

In gratitude, Cnut bestowed on the boy all the land within sound of his shepherd's horn at Pusey; although, quite how this was calculated is not recorded. To add veracity to this tale, the horn in question, a relic known as the Pusey Horn, can be seen in London's Victoria & Albert Museum.

MEDIAEVAL MAYHEM

Wallingford Castle

In the 1085 Domesday Book, Wallingford is one of only eighteen towns in the country with a population in excess of 2,000. It had been a fortified royal stronghold for 200 years already, chosen by Saxon King Alfred the Great as a place of strategic importance in his wars against the Danes. It reached its peak in the twelfth century when Empress Matilda, daughter and sole heir of King Henry I, chose Wallingford Castle as her base in the wars – 'The Anarchy' – against her usurping cousin Étienne de Blois, aka King Stephen.

The treaty that ushered in the end of the war was signed at the castle in November 1153. Stephen was to keep the throne until his death, after which it would pass to Matilda's son Henry (II). The latter didn't have to wait long, and thanked the town for its efforts by giving it a Royal Charter in 1155.

The castle and town flourished until 1349, when the population was decimated by the Black Death. The fortifications crumbled, many of its stones being incorporated into the renovated Windsor Castle. It was rebuilt by the Royalists during the English Civil War of the seventeenth century, enduring an epic sixty-five-day siege. In the aftermath, Oliver Cromwell ordered the castle – and many others, such as the ones at Oxford and Banbury – to be demolished. Some of it was translocated to the tower at St Mary-le-More Church in the town. The ruins now form a pretty pile in Wallingford Castle Gardens.

Minster Lovell House

In 1708, Lord Francis Lovell – 'Lovell the Dog' to his enemies – was discovered in a secret room at Minster Lovell House near Burford, seated at a table with book, pen, paper and faithful dog. He had been there for 221 years – trapped, after the faithful servant who locked him in inconveniently died. As the air now gushed into the deathly chamber, Lovell's and the dog's bones turned to dust.

The ruins of Minster Lovell.

Minster Lovell dovecote.

Lovell had last been seen fleeing the Battle of Stoke in 1487, having supported the pretender Lambert Simnel in his Yorkist attempt to remove the newly installed Lancastrian Tudor King Henry VII. The Earl of Oxford was instrumental in Henry's victory, and Lovell probably fled due to a pre-battle agreement of 'no quarter'. This meant that there would be no mercy on the field, i.e. no survivors. Lovell and Simnel were the only survivors of the Yorkist rebel leaders.

The fact that Minster Lovell was owned by King Henry Tudor's uncle, Jasper, makes it a very unlikely hiding spot for an anti-Tudor, and a more credible story says that Lovell escaped to Scotland and eventually won a pardon.

The notion of a fatal hiding place occurs a second time at Minster Lovell, as retold in Thomas Haynes Bayly's 1884 ballad 'The Mistletoe Bough'. Lord Lovell's young bride, during a Christmas game of hide-and-seek, finds the ideal hiding place: a large chest in the attic. In she climbs, and click goes the lock. No one finds her until many years later. This story and the hidden chamber legend are both widespread folkloric motifs.

THE OXFORDSHIRE UPRISING

On Whit Sunday 1549, the people of Bicester rose up in mass protest. The villain of the piece was a post-Catholic, post-Latin 'First Prayer Book', imposed by Henry's successor Edward VI (or, rather, by the Protestant men who formed the King's Council). Much of the country had risen in protest at Henry VIII's Dissolution of the Monasteries and the Reformation – Bicester had lost its priory in the process – with its accompanying enclosures and the inevitable economic chaos that ensued. But the English language prayer book was the last straw. The unrest that centred on this tome became known as the Oxfordshire and Buckinghamshire Uprising.

Tradition places the decisive confrontation at Enslow Hill on the Cherwell, where the rebels were persuaded to depart in peace with hollow assurances that they would not be harmed. As soon as they had retired, the King's men pursued the leaders of the uprising. A surviving letter from Lord Grey mentions that the perpetrators of the unrest were to be executed 'immediately, or else on the next market day ... and after execution done, the heads of every one of them ... to be set up in the highest place for the more terror of the said evil people.' Bicester's chief miscreant, hanged in public, was Richard Whyttington, a weaver. Three were to suffer at Oxford, three in Banbury, and two at Thame, along with single ringleaders at Watlington, Islip and Deddington. The vicars of Chipping Norton and Bloxham were hanged upon their church steeples (the former cropping up as a ghost, according to local legend). James Webbe, vicar of Barford-St-Michael, was tried in London, and then hanged, drawn and quartered in Aylesbury.

A letter written in Oxford on 7 August, by one John Ab Ulmis, reassures the status quo: '... the Oxfordshire papists are at last reduced to order, many of them having been apprehended, and some gibbeted and their heads fastened to the walls.'

THE CIVIL WAR

Banbury Mutiny

Banbury was a central base for the Parliamentarians. It was also the place where much of Charles I's gunpowder was manufactured, using saltpetre supplies from King's Sutton in Northamptonshire. The Royalists maintained a garrison at Banbury Castle, but its security became precarious as events developed. Appropriately enough, given the town's gunpowder cottage industry, the garrison was eventually overpowered and blown up by Cromwell's New Model Army.

But not all was well in the army ranks, and many became involved in the Banbury Mutiny. They criticised lack of pay and general policy from their army base in Banbury, and belonged to a wider movement soon dubbed The Levellers. Quelled, the mutineers, about 340 of them, were briefly imprisoned in Burford church, where traces of their graffiti can still be seen. 'ANTHONY SEDLEY 1649 PRISNER' is one of the most famous pieces of graffiti in the country, inscribed on the lead font. (It is an old folk belief that cutting one's name or initials in a church brings good luck, which is why old effigies in churches are so intricately defaced.)

The three perceived leaders of the mutiny were executed. Since 1975 there has been a Levellers' Day in Burford to commemorate these secular martyrs, with music, guest speakers and parades. MP Tony Benn unveiled a church wall plaque to the men in 1979.

Battle of Edgehill
In 1642, Cromwell planned the first major battle of the Civil War from his Banbury rooms in the Reindeer (now Ye Olde Reindeer Inn). It wasn't planned well, however: the Battle of Edgehill was an opportunistic and inconclusive clash, with Parliamentarians (under the Earl of Essex) marching from Warwick Castle to relieve their beleaguered Banbury garrison, and meeting the advancing Royalists on the way.

Battle of Chalgrove
The Battle of Chalgrove took place at Chalgrove Field on 18 June 1643, and was a bad day for the Earl of Essex's army. Royalist Prince Rupert had launched lightning strikes on enemy garrisons at Chinnor and Postcombe, razing the villages and then riding on to intercept a convoy carrying £21,000 in Parliamentarian army pay. The loot eluded him however, and he headed back towards Oxford (the main purpose of his attacks being to prevent Essex from approaching and blockading that Royalist city).

One of Essex's leading players, Colonel John Hampden, pursued Rupert's troublemakers, and the forces met at Chalgrove – where Rupert had halted in order to set an ambush. Rupert's ploy failed, and in typical derring-do mode he switched to Plan B, leaping over the hedge that separated the two forces to lead his men into battle. It was the kind of stuff that brought him fame, short-lived though his star proved to be.

Rupert won the day at Chalgrove, and things couldn't have gone worse for poor Hampden. Levelling his pistol at the enemy, the weapon exploded in his hand, mortally wounding him. He returned home to Thame, where he died of his injuries six days later. It was a huge setback for the Parliamentarians, and Essex even offered to resign. The offer was not accepted.

Battle of Culham Bridge
The Royalists occupied Culham Bridge as part of their Abingdon encampment. But in 1644, Cromwell's men commandeered it as a base from which to attack Royalist supply lines to Charles I's headquarters at Oxford. In the following year, the Battle of Culham Bridge saw Royalist commander Sir Henry Gage mortally wounded after a failed attempt to recapture and destroy the crossing.

Battle of Cropredy Bridge
'Site of the Battle of Cropredy Bridge. From Civil War Deliver Us,' reads a plaque on the bridge at Cropredy. The battle took place in 1644, the Parliamentarians suffering heavy losses but winning a stalemate (if such a thing is possible). The confrontation has inspired at least two songs, written nearly 350 years after the event. 'Scarecrow' by Steeleye Span emerged in 1984, followed by 'Red and Gold' by Ralph McTell a few years later, written for the Cropredy-based band Fairport Convention.

Oxford University
Oxford split down its natural fault line in the wars, the Town supporting the Parliamentarians, and the University staunchly Royalist. As the University wielded all the real power, the city became King Charles I's stronghold during the hostilities. He set up a camp-cum-court at Christ Church College between 1642 and 1646, and his Queen Henrietta Maria made her home at Merton.

Oxford was eventually besieged by Cromwell's army in 1646, and when Oliver became Chancellor of the University in 1650, he replaced many Royalist University men with his own hand-picked team. And just to show who was boss, he ordered

Christ Church staircase.

the city to be 'slighted', which entailed destroying its castle defences. This is why today's Castle Mound has no castle.

During the siege, a gang of 'Roaring Cavaliers in a fiddling prophane Ale-house' (to quote a pro-Parliamentarian report) lost control of their hog roast, the flames torching the area between George Street and Queen Street, and causing more damage to the city than the armed conflict itself.

Cromwell House
While the Royalists defended Oxford, the Parliamentarians established base at Marston (now an Oxford suburb). It is said that Oliver Cromwell visited military mastermind Thomas Fairfax here at 17 Mill Lane, now known as Cromwell House. Fairfax used to spy on the enemy's artillery and defences from the tower of St Nicholas' Church, gazing across to the University Parks area of the city. When the fighting was over in 1646, the Treaty for the Surrender of Oxford was signed at the Mill Lane house.

Radley
The church at Radley near Abingdon was battered during a skirmish in the wars, and dents in the door, made by irate locked-out Parliamentarians, can still be seen. (This was not to be the last of its physical tribulations either: it was closed between June 2008 and February 2009 while repairs took place to mend the damage caused by an infestation of death watch beetle.)

William Lenthall
One of Radley church's benefactors, William Lenthall, blew with the winds of the time: he took up the Parliamentarian cause in the wars, and was Speaker on several occasions before, during and after the conflict (in which he maintained a pro-Charles I stance wherever possible). Not so much because of his great skills, but because he was a proven puppet. He even managed to escape with his life when Charles II took the throne, having supported the Restoration after Cromwell's death and pointing out that he had sent aid to the beleaguered Queen in Oxford during the Civil War.

Lenthall was banned from holding further public office after the Restoration, retiring to his grand piles at Burford Priory and Besselsleigh Manor, dying at the latter on 9 November 1662. His on-the-fence role in history seems to have preyed on his conscience. In his will, he requested that he be buried with neither pomp nor monument, 'acknowledging myself to be unworthy of the least outward regard in this world and unworthy of any remembrance that hath been so great a sinner'. Instead, he asked for a plain stone carved with the Latin inscription *Vermis sum*, meaning 'I am a worm'.

Henry Marten

Henry Marten, seventeenth-century resident of Oxford and Beckett Hall in Shrivenham, believed that the monarchy should be abolished. He was sufficiently outspoken in his republican ideas to earn a stint in the Tower of London. No one was more surprised than him when his wish actually came true: Marten was one of the 'regicides' who signed the death warrant of Charles I after the Royalists' defeat in the English Civil Wars.

Marten was a man of contradictions. An avowed Puritan, he was also renowned for his love of drink and loose women, squandering much of his fortune on the two vices. Indeed, Charles I had condemned him as a 'whoremaster', which did little to bend Marten's views in his favour. Even more surprisingly, this regicide is also said to have considered assassinating Oliver Cromwell. After the Restoration, irate King Charles II banished Marten from his lands at Shrivenham (which was in Berkshire prior to 1974). He died in 1680 at Chepstow, after choking on his supper.

WAR AND DEATH IN THE TWENTIETH CENTURY

Airman's Bridge

A former toll bridge – now known as the Airman's Bridge – crosses the Thames at Wolvercote. It has a plaque commemorating an accident which took place in 1912, when the adjoining Port Meadow was a military airfield. Two officers of the Royal Flying Corps were killed when their plane crashed, and 2,226 Oxfordians gave money to have the plaque installed.

Sutton Courtenay

Sutton Courtenay, near Abingdon, has the very dubious honour of being the place where Britain's part in the First World War formally began. Prime Minister Herbert Asquith, educated at Balliol College in Oxford and later given the title Lord Oxford, had bought Walton House on the edge of the village in 1912, building his main residence – The Wharf – next door. Here he signed the declaration that plunged the country into conflict. Asquith remained in the village after his resignation in 1916, and is buried there in All Saints' churchyard.

The church itself dates back to the twelfth century; but it nearly closed its doors prematurely during the English Civil Wars in the seventeenth century. The vicar at the time stored munitions for the Parliamentarians, and had to cancel services when the stash exploded, taking a large chunk of the church with it.

Westwell

The thirteenth-century Lakenhalle or Cloth Hall at Ypres in Belgium, the largest commercial building of the Middle Ages, was flattened during artillery fire in the First World War. After the war, one of the Roman 'I' numerals from the hall's shattered tower clock made its way to Westwell near Burford, where Lady Stetta Aimee Holland, wife of the Lord of the Manor at Westwell, incorporated it into the war memorial beside the picturesque village pond. The memorial was specifically in memory of her brothers Harold and John Price, who had been killed during the war. However, other than their sister, the Prices had no connection with Westwell.

Members of the Oxfordshire and Buckinghamshire Light Infantry had taken part in the bitter First Battle of Ypres, 1914, along with the equally devastating Battle of Passchendaele near Ypres in 1917. The memorial is an apt reminder of this connection.

Caversfield

Although its history stretches back to before the Norman Conquest, Caversfield's population had seldom reached three figures until 1911, when Bicester Airfield (later RAF Bicester) installed servicemen on Skimmington Lane. The RAF moved out in 2004 and the old houses are now used by the MOD's Defence Logistics Organisation, which has since become part of an amalgamated organisation, Defence Equipment & Support. Airmen from the US Air Force, based at RAF Croughton in Northamptonshire, live in the parish too.

The second big shock to the system was the expansion of Bicester's suburbs, some of which have been allocated to the Caversfield parish.

Begbroke

During the Second World War, Begbroke had a unique unit of Air Raid Precautions (ARP) wardens, made up of Servite friars. They were based at the eighteenth-century Begbroke Manor House, which had become part of the Roman Catholic Priory of St Philip in the 1880s (remaining a base for novice Servite friars until 2000). The brethren could boast hotline prayers as well as sharp eyes amongst their anti-air raid armoury.

There were also Servite would-be nuns in Begbroke until 1984, when St Juliana's Convent School closed due to structural issues and cash-flow problems. It was the kind of financial bomb and structural damage that not even the holy ARPs could have assisted with.

Benson

The clock on the 1794 church tower at Benson is marked out in Roman numerals, and has XI at both the 11 and the 9 positions. This error was exploited to fiendish effect by Irish-raised American British Union of Fascists member William Joyce, aka Lord Haw-Haw, in the Second World War. Working for Nazi Germany's English-language propaganda programme, *Germany Calling*, Joyce announced to a cowed Britain that there would be an air raid on 'an airfield near the village whose clock has two elevens'. Riddle-busters failed to crack the code, and RAF Benson was bombed.

Hatford

During the Second World War, Hatford's off-licence received a direct hit from a German bomb. A girl was killed in the blast, along with two boys from London. With the darkest of irony, they had been evacuated here to escape the London Blitz.

Oxford

It is said that Hitler ensured that no bombs fell on Oxford, so that he could use it as his base following German victory in the Second World War.

Barford-St-John

The RAF base at Barford-St-John only lasted four years – between 1942 and 1946 – but the site has since been taken over by the United States Air Force, which has a communications centre on the old airfield, linked to the enormously numbered 2,130th Communications Squadron at RAF Croughton in Northamptonshire. From this base, the USAF deals with an estimated one third of all the USA's military communications in Europe.

Wallingford

Wallingford was saved from disaster in 1944 by self-sacrificing airmen. When a Royal Canadian Air Force Halifax bomber caught fire whilst flying over the town, most of the crew bailed out. But Flying Officer Wilding and Sergeant Andrew stayed onboard. The aircraft was carrying its full capacity of bombs, and would have left a large hole in the town. The suicide mission steered the flaming plane in a nose-dive to an isolated field near Crowmarsh. An obelisk at the junction of Wilding Road and Andrew Road in Wallingford commemorates the event.

Berinsfield

Berinsfield was founded in 1957, the first new village in England for 200 years. It was on the site of RAF Mount Farm, originally a satellite of RAF Benson, and later a base for the United States Army Air Force. Glenn Miller performed here for American troops shortly before hopping over to RAF Twinwood, and from there to his appointment with death, famously lifting off in a small aircraft on his way to the troops in Paris in December 1944, and never seen again.

Bullingdon Rural District Council was in charge of the development of the new village, and they named it after local saint Berin, adding the 'field' bit to reflect the fact that it had been an American airfield. The first residents had to make do with the old air base huts, until the work of architect William Holford reached fruition in 1960.

Brize Norton

Brize Norton may well have a venerable history stretching back to the Saxons, but today it says just one thing to most people: the RAF, based here since 1937. Indeed, RAF Brize Norton is the largest station in the Royal Air Force, employing 4,500 people. The station has been busy over the last couple of decades, as it is the main airport used for deploying UK troops worldwide. In the current century, the military operations in Iraq and Afghanistan have required its services far more often than anyone would like.

Its mission is 'to protect Air Transport and Air-to-Air Refuelling and support deployed operations and exercises'. Vickers VC10s (101 Squadron), L-1011 TriStars (216 Squadron) and Boeing C-17 Globemasters (99 Squadron) are the main aircraft, key rapid response machinery in both national and NATO defence strategy. Parachute training is another important aspect of the work going on here.

In 2012, after the restructuring known as Programme Future Brize, the station welcomed the entire RAF Hercules force, along with new Atlas and Voyager craft. After the closure of RAF Lyneham, Brize Norton became the sole station for the embarkation of British troops. Its fleet of craft has risen from thirty to seventy as a result.

Faringdon

In the 1940s, a member of the Home Guard in Faringdon mixed some Molotov Cocktails, to be used in the event of the Germans marching in. He then buried the cache in his cottage, on land now covered by the Community College (formerly Tollington School), and promptly forgot all about it.

In 1974 the cache was discovered, and demonstrated that it would indeed have hindered the invaders: one of the bottles smashed and its phosphorus instantly caught fire. A bomb disposal team from Hounslow defused the DIY bombs, and the war was finally over.

Sir Stafford Cripps

A tiny museum of bygones relating to the splendidly titled villages of Filkins and Broughton Poggs is kept in a seventeenth-century cottage in Filkins. It is called the Swinford Museum, after its founder George, who established it in the 1930s with the help of Labour MP Sir Stafford Cripps (who lived locally).

Cripps was one of the politicians who welcomed a Soviet delegation of jet engine designers in 1946, who were seeking help with their faltering projects back home in the USSR. Sir Stafford, with a benevolent nod from his Party, allowed them to study Rolls Royce jet engine technology, and discussed a licence by which they could produce versions of the engine for Soviet planes. This resulted in the Klimov VK-1 jet engine, used in the MiG-15s that fought against UN forces in North Korea in the 1950s, much to the dismay of the B-29 bombers they targeted.

All of this had come as a great shock to Josef Stalin. When his jet engineers first approached him with the proposal to contact the UK in 1946, Stalin is reputed to have responded: 'But what fool will sell us his secrets?'

Little Baldon and Toot Baldon

Peacetime is not without its casualties. Little Baldon near Oxford was the scene of an air disaster on 6 July 1965, when a No. 36 Squadron RAF transport aircraft took off from Abingdon, en route to RAF Benson, and crashed into a field near Little Baldon. Forty-one people onboard were killed, and the tall crops made searching for bodies difficult. An inquest implicated metal fatigue in some of the aircraft's bolts.

There is a commemorative plaque in the Church of St Lawrence at Toot Baldon, and a service of remembrance is held every July.

David Kelly

In 2006, Thom Yorke of rock band Radiohead recorded the song 'Harrowdown Hill' for his solo album *The Eraser*. It is an angry rant about David Kelly, who was found dead on Harrowdown, near Longworth, in 2003 at the height of the Weapons of Mass Destruction investigation in the second Gulf War. The death was also the subject of 2010 Turner Prize nominee Dexter Dalwood's painting *Death of David Kelly* in 2008.

Kelly's critical comments regarding the Government's behaviour, primarily the dubious quality of its intelligence gathering, had leaked into the media. The ensuing pressure made him turn to suicide, according to the official verdict. Thom Yorke, Dexter Dalwood and several others saw matters differently, sniffing a whole different kind of scandal.

BIBLIOGRAPHY

Illustration credits:

Ditchfield, P.H. (ed.), *Memorials of Old Oxfordshire* (Bemrose & Sons, London, 1903)

Evans, Herbert A., *Highways and Byways in Oxford and the Cotswolds*, illustrated by Frederick L. Griggs (Macmillan and Co., London, 1908)

Freeborn, M.E., *'Twixt Cherwell and Glyme* (Simpkin, Marshall, Hamilton, Kent & Co., London, 1900)

Spiers, R.A.H. (compiler) *Round About 'The Mitre' at Oxford (Episodes of the University, City and Hotel)*, (The Mitre, Oxford, 1929)

Wells, J., *The Charm of Oxford*, new edition, illustrations by W.G. Blackwell (Simpkin Marshall Ltd, London, 1934)

Books:

Oxford During the Last Century: being two series of papers published in the Oxford Chronicle & Berks & Bucks Gazette during the year 1859 (Slatter and Rose, Oxford, 1859)

Anon., *History, Gazeteer and Directory of the County of Oxford* (Robert Gardner, Peterborough, 1852)

Bompas, G.C., *Life of Frank Buckland* (Smith, Elder & Co., London, 1886)

Clark, Andrew (ed.), *Survey of the Antiquities of the City of Oxford, composed in 1661–6, by Anthony Wood* (Clarendon Press, Oxford, 1889)

Davies, K.C. and J. Hull, *The Zoological Collections of the Oxford University Museum* (Oxford University Museum, 1976)

Foxe, John, *Foxe's Book of Martyrs* (London, 1563)

Gaspard Brabant, Frederick, *Oxfordshire* (Methuen, London, 1919)

House, J., *Geography of Oxfordshire* (Collins, London, 1870)

Marriott Davenport, John, *Oxfordshire Annals* (E.W. Morris, Oxford, 1869)

Meade Falkner, John, *A History of Oxfordshire* (London, 1899)

Morris, Jan, *Oxford* (OUP, 1978)

Morris, Jan, *The Oxford Book of Oxford* (OUP, 1978)

Murray, John, *A Handbook for Travellers in Berks, Bucks, and Oxfordshire* (John Murray, London, 1860)

Pevsner, Nikolaus and Jennifer Sherwood, *The Buildings of England: Oxfordshire* (Harmondsworth, London, 1974)

Plot, Robert, *The Natural History of Oxfordshire* (Oxford, 1677)

Sullivan, Paul, *Oxford: A Pocket Miscellany* (The History Press, Stroud, 2011)

Tuckwell, W., *Reminiscences of Oxford* (E.P. Dutton & Co., New York, 1901)

Walker, Revd John, *Oxoniana: or Anecdotes Relative to the University and City of Oxford* (Slatter & Munday, Oxford, 1806)

Warton, Thomas, *Specimen of a History of Oxfordshire* (London, 1783)

Whittock, Nathaniel, *Description of the University and City of Oxford* (Isaac Taylor Hinton, London, 1828)

Wood, Anthony and Thomas Hearne, *The Life of Anthony à Wood From the Year 1632 to 1672* (Clarendon Press, Oxford, 1772)

Woodforde, James, ed. John Beresford, *The Diary of a Country Parson, 1758–1802* (OUP 1978)

Newspapers and journals:

Banbury Guardian (Banbury)
Bicester Advertiser (Bicester)
Burlington Magazine for Connoisseurs (London)
Folklore (London)
Jackson's Oxford Journal (Oxford)
Notes & Queries (Oxford)
Oxford Mail (Oxford)
Oxfordshire Limited Edition (Oxford)
Oxford Times (Oxford)
Oxford Today (Oxford)
Past & Present (Oxford)
Social History (Lancaster)

Websites:

en.wikipedia.org
news.bbc.co.uk/1/hi/england/Oxfordshire
www.banburyshireinfo.co.uk
www.bbc.co.uk/oxford
www.bbowt.org.uk
www.berkshirehistory.com
www.british-history.ac.uk
www.dailyinfo.co.uk
www.faringdon.org
www.headington.org.uk
www.inoxfordmag.co.uk
www.oum.ox.ac.uk (University Museum of Natural History)
www.ox.ac.uk/colleges (University and Colleges portal)
www.oxfordcityguide.com
www.oxford.gov.uk
www.oxfordshirecotswolds.org
www.oxfordshire.gov.uk
www.megalithic.co.uk
www.nationaltrust.org.uk
www.naturalengland.org.uk
www.paintedchurch.org
www.paranormaldatabase.com
www.shotover.clara.net
www.wildcru.org
www.wychwood.co.uk
www.wychwoodproject.org